RYE'S WAR

1939 - 1945
The Second World War in Rye

Edited by Josephine C. Kirkham

Published by Rye Museum Association

First Published March 2002

ISBN0-905253-04-3

Published by the Rye Museum Association
3 East Street, Rye
East Sussex. TN31 7JY

Printed by The Chameleon Press Ltd.
5 - 25 Burr Road, Wandsworth
London. SW18 4SG

CONTENTS

ILLUSTRATIONS

Foreword

Writing an account of 'Rye's War' is a daunting and complicated task. There are the facts of what happened in Europe; there are chronological lists of events in the Town itself, when of course Rye was part of the home front line for Britain, and thus nationally important, and there are the interesting and wonderful individual stories of the people who were in the town and surrounding area during the war. These last accounts can sometimes repeat the same incident, but all have something different to say. I must apologise for editing some of theses incidents out, so that the incident itself appears only once, but I have tried to present different views and perceptions of the same incidents on occasions.

Putting it all together has given a wonderful picture of Rye in the dark days of 1939-45. I must thank all local people who talked to the young people of Thomas Peacocke Community College Local History Group over the years for the Rye Memories Series, and many of these recollections are being published for the first time.

We have had, and are still receiving, so many contributions that there is not enough room to include them all in this volume and so a second and even maybe a third, may be produced. If readers of this book have any memories, please do send them in, or contact the Museum.

This book not only came out of the work done at Thomas Peacocke, but also from the decision to hold an exhibition on the Second World War at Rye Castle Museum. The book is intended both to support and enhance the exhibition. There is so much to say and so many stories to tell. The illustrations try to show just how much Rye was physically changed by the war. The town did change slowly over the years, but the important features and feel of the town had remained largely intact over the previous two hundred years. However, Rye's position on the 'Front Line' resulted in much bomb damage, which dramatically changed large parts of the town.

I would like to give particular thanks to: Maurice Blackman, Clifford Bloomfield, David Cade, Alan Catt, Colin Cooke, Rosalie Eldrid, Audrey Hatter, Sheila Miller, Betty Paine, Frank Palmer, Cecilie Prebble, Frank Reeve, Doris Scotcher, Joan Sherwood, and the late Jack Matthews and P.C.Moppett for their contributions to this volume. Clifford Bloomfield's recollections did appear in 'Wings Over Rye', but it has been edited and added to for this publication.

I am also grateful to Shirley Brinkhurst, Rosalind Collier, Brian Hargreaves and Pauline Kingswood for all their help in recording and finding new memories and in many other ways, Joyce Hargreaves for the meticulous care and attention she has taken in ensuring the book was brought together for the printers, and also Brian Hargreaves and Clifford Bloomfield for their illustrations. Allan Downend, Curator of Rye Castle Museum, has been, as always, immensely supportive.

Jo Kirkham   January 2002

To the people of Rye who have so often throughout their history,
been on the 'Front Line' in the defence of our country:
may it never have to occur again.

INTRODUCTION

Rye in Late 1939

Rye's population in 1939 was about 4,500 and the Corporation ran the Borough, led by the Mayor, Aldermen and Councillors. It employed Officers such as the Town Clerk, Borough Surveyor, Treasurer, Medical Officer of Health and a workforce. These were to maintain highways, (except the classified roads) and houses which it owned; water supply from wells under Cadborough, the Water Works on Military Road, and the Rye Hill Tower; sewage disposal - it ran straight into the river system and hopefully out to sea on the outgoing tide; and refuse collection - which was buried in certain marsh fields and covered.

In 1939, an Air Raid Precautions Organisation, consisting of Councillors, A.R.P. officers and Medical personnel, was added to the 14 other Borough Committees: its job was to prepared to defend Rye.

All Courts of Justice were held in the Town Hall: Quarter Sessions for serious cases, and Magistrates Courts on Mondays and Wednesdays. These were busy in the War.

Education in Rye was at the Grammar School; the Senior School in New Road; the Junior School in Lion Street until Christmas 1939, and then in Ferry Road; the Rye Collegiate School on Hilder's Cliff, and the Rye Evening Institute.

The Post Office, also the Telephone Exchange, was open for Telegrams until 9 pm and the Letter Box was cleared 11 times daily.

The Rye Gas and Coke Co. Ltd was where the Kettle of Fish and car park is now. Electricity was supplied from Hastings.

There were many individual shopkeepers and tradesmen which

made Rye virtually self-sufficient. The Cattle Market was busy and many women were employed 'in Domestic Service'.

Public Transport was vital. Rye was served daily by 21 trains, 11 bus services and the Camber Tram. It also had 16 Carriers, Haulage Contractors and motors for hire.

Several large works provided employment, such as Rother Iron Works and Spun Concrete. The Harbour's main business was fishing, but coal and timber still came by sea. H.M. Customs House was at 2 High Street.

There were 7 places of worship in the Borough: the Parish Church of St Mary; the Baptist Church; the Congregational Church, the Bethel Strict Baptist; the Methodist Church; the Roman Catholic Church, St Anthony of Padua; and the Salvation Army. These played a large part in the life of Ryers and later the service personnel.

It had well organised health - welfare services. The Registrar of Births, Marriages and Deaths also performed weddings. Rye and District Memorial Hospital was vital and about £1.900 a year was raised to keep it going. Nurses could be hired for home care. Other welfare clubs were The British Legion, the Christmas Cheer Fund, Toc H, 12 Birthday Clubs, 2 Thrift Clubs, and 8 Benefit Societies. Ryers always raised money for charities, and later the wartime appeals.

Rye Borough Fire Brigade, with 15 members, had its H.Q. in the new Fire Station, Ferry Road. Sub-Stations were the Old Fire Station (Town Hall) and Bryan's Garage. An air-raid system was fitted to the station's hose tower and 2 more sirens were later put on the Landgate and the Martello Tower in Winchelsea Road.

The Police Force consisted of an Inspector, 4 Constables in Rye, 10 in the Villages, and a Keeper of the Lock-up.

The St John Ambulance and the Red Cross also did vital work. St John's ran the Rye and District Motor Ambulance and a Civil Defence Ambulance augmented this when war began.

The Territorial Army flourished with its H.Q. in the Drill Hall in Mill Lane.

Rye had a huge number of leisure activities, which were soon affected by the War; members were called up and facilities commandeered. Most families rented an allotment from the Corporation, on North Salts, on land behind South Undercliff, and on St Mary's Marsh by the Grammar School, producing vegetables.

The Civilian population was encouraged to join classes on first-aid, gas warfare and civil defence and to volunteer to be Air-Raid Wardens, Local Defence Volunteers (later Home Guard), Auxiliary Firemen, Special Police Constables, and in the Women's Voluntary Service. Ryers responded in huge numbers, modifying their activities to help the War effort. The locals played a full part in defending their town, and Britain, and welcomed many service men and women who joined them. Rye experienced a lot of war activity, being on the Front Line once war was declared and, in some respects, had a vital position. Here are some stories of this very special place in a unique period of Britain's history.

Tank traps on Rye Hill.

The War: A Brief Timeline

1939: The fear of War built throughout the year and Emergency Preparations were made in Rye and district.
3 SEPTEMBER: Britain's ultimatum to Germany expired at 11 am. Most people remembered where they were, when they listened to the radio to hear Prime Minister Neville Chamberlain report that we were 'at war'. Immediately after this, Rye's Sirens sounded. People were frightened and ran for cover. Some put the lessons in Gas Warfare and Civil Defence into action. Buckets of water were filled, soaked blankets were hung over doors and windows, food collected together; and then the All Clear sounded - it was a false alarm.
SEPTEMBER 1939 - APRIL 1940: The Phoney War. The British Expeditionary Force, including many Rye soldiers, was in France. Hitler was in Poland and life in Rye continued much as before, but with constant War preparations. Children from London were evacuated to Rye. Gas masks had to be carried.
1940: 16 - 29 JANUARY 1940: Very heavy snow, drifts 8 - 12 feet deep on Romney Marsh. Trains stopped; Troops under canvas suffered badly; killed sheep and schools were closed in Rye.
2 APRIL: German planes flew low over the Marsh and Rye.
APRIL 1940: Germany captured Denmark, and invaded Norway, Holland and Belgium. Some Rye men in the B.E.F. were captured and became P.O.W.'s, as they withdrew to the Dunkirk beaches. Spitfire landed.

Anti-invasion precautions taken as our beaches would be the landing point; building gun emplacements, tank traps and underground petrol tanks ready to set the sea on fire, putting up barbed wire, wood and metal 'hedgehogs', and building large block houses like those at Rye Harbour Road and Camber to prevent the Germans getting inland. Many guns were installed around Rye.
10 MAY: Winston Churchill became Prime Minister and told Parliament to get ready for "Hard and heavy tidings!"
26 MAY - 3 JUNE: 'Operation Dynamo': Several Rye boats, includ-

ing the Mizpah, helped the successful evacuation of about 340,000 British and French soldiers from the beaches at Dunkirk. Trains full of exhausted men passed through the Town from the Dover area.

From this time the Rye area was 'The Front' - with Germany occupying the whole of the French Coast only 40 miles away. The Royal Military Canal was to be defended, and barbed wire was put along its inland side. The Local Defence Volunteers became a vital force.

JULY: L.D.V. renamed the Home Guard. Their only uniform was denim overalls and a forage cap. They had no proper arms either - just a few odd rifles collected from local sources and things from home like shot guns and pitchforks. The Home Guard Auxiliary Service or 'Secret Army' was also being established in Iden (actually Peasmarsh) and Icklesham. A.R.P.; Auxiliary Firemen, Special Constables, Air Raid Wardens and the Observer Corps, all practiced their skills.

JULY - AUGUST - SEPTEMBER: Imminent danger of invasion.

1 JULY: King George VI visited Rye to see the coastal defences and lunched at the George.

10 JULY:Battle of Britain begins.

16 JULY:Hitler orders preparations for invading Britain - "Operation Sea Lion", to beach thousands of soldiers, tanks etc in landing craft between Dungeness and Fairlight, to be completed by mid August.

21 JULY: Most children, some with teachers or mothers, but others alone were evacuated to Bedford, Somerset and South Wales.

30 JULY: Duke of Gloucester visited Rye and Lydd.

AUGUST AND SEPTEMBER: The Battle of Britain intensified and was fought in the skies above Rye. Ryers watched the vapour trails and dog fights daily. The Home Guard patrolled the Town side of the rivers and Regular Soldiers manned the entrances to the town, the bridges and the gun sites. Identity Cards had to be shown when passing checkpoints. Air raid shelters had been built around the Town for refuge from air attack. The Royal Engineers laid thousands of land mines.

Ryers watched as the Radar Station at Brookland was bombed twice. Some deaths were caused, but with little damage to the Radar itself; it was working again within three hours. Some Germans, from crashed planes, were taken to Rye Hospital.

18 AUGUST: Rye had its first bombing when 28 bombs landed on the Town killing 3 people in Wish Ward and injuring others. Raids continued. Lamb House Garden Room destroyed.

20 AUGUST: Churchill gave his "so much owed to so few' speech.

SEPTEMBER: Government change of plan - decided to defend the Marsh.

2 SEPTEMBER:Mayor opens Spitfire Fund.

3-4 SEPTEMBER: 4 spies came ashore on the Marsh beaches and soon captured. Many planes crashed on the Marshes around Rye.

16 SEPTEMBER: The RAF had virtually won the Battle of Britain.

19 SEPTEMBER:Operation Sea Lion put on ice. Hitler turned to Russia. German raids continued - more at night - the Blitz.

9 OCTOBER: Another serious bombing attack on Rye, when 18 50-kilo bombs were dropped, causing much damage.

17 DECEMBER: Wellington bomber crashed in Kings Avenue after running out of fuel.

1941: German patrols raided Rye when pilots machine gunned, dropped bombs and incendiaries. Many planes on returning from bombing raids in London, dumped their final bombs on Rye and Romney Marsh. Various Regiments came and went - the soldiers often making lasting friendships with Rye people. The Home Guard continued to have many exercises.

24 OCTOBER: Rye Borough Council's first contact with Minesweeper H.M.S. Rye.

1942: 9 MARCH: Town adopts H.M.S. Rye.

SEPTEMBER : 'Hit and Run' attacks against the Rye area became even worse.

15 SEPTEMBER: Raid damaged a lot of buildings, including the rear of the Mermaid Inn.

16 SEPTEMBER: The 'Mizpah,' attacked whilst fishing in Rye Bay, had 2 crew killed and the skipper wounded.

22 SEPTEMBER: Raid killed 3 and injured workmen, busy making

safe buildings from the raid a week earlier. Other bombs destroyed the Regent Cinema, (killing the Manager) and damaging the Methodist Chapel and Ypres Castle.

7 OCTOBER: A bomb dropped on a Rye Harbour house killed 2 ladies.

21 OCTOBER: A Beaufighter was shot down by 'friendly fire'.

6 DECEMBER: Machine guns from 2 German planes killed 1 on the Ypres Steps and injured others in the Town.

1943: 15 JANUARY: 5 German planes flew along the old cliff line east to west, dropping bombs, cannon and machine gunning.

10 FEBRUARY: Another heavy "tip and run" raid from Tillingham Avenue to the Strand killed 2, injured others and did much damage.

31 MARCH: Auxiliary Coastguard John Southerden's prompt action saved the crew of the 'Caulonia' off Jury's Gap. He alerted the Hastings Lifeboat and soldiers.

6 SEPTEMBER: Flying Fortresses arrived back, shot to pieces.

11 DECEMBER: Ack Ack fire brought a German plane down near Rye. Its bombs exploded and all died.

BY END OF 1943: A camouflaged oil pipeline, 'PLUTO' was built from Walton-on-Thames to Dungeness for 'Operation Overlord'; one branch went from Brookland to the Rye Harbour railhead, going west of the Golf Club House and under the River Rother; 15 large tanks were put in the Camber dunes.

1944. EARLY 1944: Our fighters practised aiming at targets off Rye Harbour before bombing northern France; much Civil Engineering at the Harbour for the Royal Navy and the Camber Tram ran again; Mosquitoes and Ack Ack fire continued to bring down German planes.

JANUARY: Mosquitoes and Ack Ack fire continued to bring down German planes.

4 FEBRUARY: General Montgomery inspected many of the Troops on the Cricket Salts in Rye.

21 MARCH: Training for D Day; heavy guns and tanks on Lydd Ranges; exercises on Camber Sands; and Naval ships watched practice landings.

13 MAY:Winston Churchill and other dignitaries inspected the Troops being assembled for D Day in Rye, Wittersham, Brede and Battle.
6 JUNE: D Day, the invasion of Europe.
13 JUNE: A new aircraft was noticed with flames coming out of the tail. Hitler's Secret Weapon, the V I, Flying Bomb or 'doodlebug,' moved faster than our planes could fly and was difficult to shoot down on its way to bomb London. Several lanes of these V I's came across the Channel actually over our area.

Mothers and children were again evacuated from the Town. Eventually some of our pilots learned a new techniques of hitting the "doodlebugs wing" and thus changing their course so they would crash. Big guns in huge numbers were placed along the shore from Winchelsea Beach, Rye Harbour to Camber, with 1300 gunners including the RAF Regiment, who also devised techniques to stop them.

Shooting the VI's down, however, meant danger for Rye, and 7 doodlebugs came down within the Borough causing casualties and much damage. Many more came down in the nearby marshes. At the height of the Flying Bomb attack, the night barrage was spectacular, with the bombs themselves, the planes, the big guns and the searchlights swinging their beams around the sky.
28 JULY: A 'doodlebug', hit by Ack Ack, came down in Camber and demolished the Church, village hall etc. Huge numbers of 'Doodles' were seen and felt for 6 weeks.
30 AUGUST: The 'doodlebug' menace ended.

By Christmas 1944: The number of bombs dropped as the British toll on German bombers increased. This is when the children evacuated in 1940 with the Grammar School, and those sent away for a second time at the start of the 'doodlebug' threat, returned to Rye.
1945: 20 APRIL: Blackout restrictions were lifted.
7 MAY: The invasion of Europe by the Allies on all fronts had been successful.
8 MAY: The WAR ended.
9 MAY: A holiday!

Home Guard

Four days after Winston Churchill became Prime Minister on 10 May 1940, Anthony Eden asked men between 17 and 45 to enrol in the Local Defence Volunteers; a military force, intended mainly to deal with paratroop landings behind the main lines. To enrol they reported to the local Police Station. They were renamed the Home Guard in July.

The Rye Company, (later Q), had its first Headquarters in the old school in Mermaid Street. The ranges and equipment of the Rye Miniature Rifle Club, in the same building, were handed over to the Company. Many of the men had to be given instruction on how to handle a rifle.

Divided into five sections or platoons, they were, at first, commanded by Cyril Tolley, a famous golfer, then Captain H. Plews. Each section was made responsible for a particular area. No. 1 Platoon was in charge of Rye Town, and, by August, it had 60 men; the whole Company was 200 strong. George Cade was appointed Quarter Master and the other officers included F.D.Hinds, H.D.A.Watney, H.Catt, J.A.Saunders and W.B.Hacking. The last was later killed by a flying bomb in 1944.

Other members included: C.Ades, J.Allen, F. Arnold, R. Bailey, E.Bannister, A. Bartholomew, H.Blackman, H.Booth, S.Bourne, W.Bray, W.Bryan, F.Bryant, F.Bumsted, A.Case, E.Clark, H.Cloute, C.Cotterell, C.Coveney, B.Cutting, G.Dawson, C.Dobbie, Donovan, J.Edwards, H.Elliott, C.Forsdyke, A.Gibbs, W.Gibbs, L.Giles, J. Goodwin, H.Hall, H.Hobbs, E.Huckstep, C.Kingsmill, E.Laurence, R.McKechnie, D.Miles, P.Miles, A.Milton, E.Noakes, E.Odell, S.Oyler, H.Page, H.Parker, Mr Parsons, H.Phillips, H.dePree, D.Reed, E.Robins, F.Scragg, D.Sewett, G.Sim, F.Sinden, M.Sinden, G.Smith, F.Smith, J.Southerden, W.Southerden, E.Standen, F.Swann, H.Talbot, S.Tiltman, V.Terry, C.Tolley, R.Weeks, W.Willoughby and R.Wyborn.

At first No 1 platoon provided the sentries for Carter's Works at Rye Harbour and Rye Post Office in the High Street. Firing classes were held at the Camber Castle Range, lectures were given on the use of firearms, and drills were held on the Salts.

In November they moved to new, larger Headquarters in the Drill Hall in Windmill Lane and guards were posted there every night. This building was demolished in 1987.

Initially they were short of weapons, ammunition and other equipment. The first uniform was army denim with field service caps. Canadian and American rifles were delivered in September.

In 1941, battle dress replaced the denim overalls and by then they were almost fully equipped.

Mock battles took place and, in May 1941, Phillips Boatyard in Rock Channel was the site of one of these. In a thunderstorm in May 1942, the Company defending Queen's Well, in Deadman's Lane, drove back an attack by the Durham Light Infantry, with blank ammunition.

Another time was when the Company attacked some men from Peasmarsh who pretended to be German paratroopers, at Marley Farm. By 1942, the men were fully trained and equipped, but their duties were reduced to defending the Drill Hall, Post Office and Martello Tower in Winchelsea Road.

Many of the men had much experience to offer, as they were Great War veterans.

At the end of the War they received a card from King George VI saying "*In the years when our country was in mortal danger ..... gave generously of his time to make himself ready for her defence by force of arms and with his life if need be.*"

PEAR SHAPED CONCRETE ROAD blocks.

The British Secret Resistance

This was organised as Home Guard Auxiliary Units, the title hiding its real purpose of a British Resistance Movement. Launched in March 1938, the Units were part of the Secret Service.

The evacuation of Dunkirk, when invasion was a real danger, gave an impetus to the scheme's development. Colonel C. Gubbins had chosen 12 intelligence officers, each to be in charge of a section of coast, and these chose their own junior officers, N.C.O.'s and training personnel.

Col. Gubbins used the Home Guard as a basis, for many members were young men who were in reserved occupations. All possible members were vetted by the Police and supposed to sign the Official Secrets act. The units were to be of small numbers of specially trained men, and their aim was to be able to sabotage behind German lines and gather intelligence if invasion occurred.

It was organised in three sections over Britain, Scotland 201, Northern England 202 and Southern England, who became the 203rd Battalion of the Home Guard. The 203 consisted of Kent, Sussex, Hampshire, Dorset, Somerset, Devon and Cornwall. Not officially recognised, the Geneva Convention would not have covered them and, if caught, they would have been shot! Their life expectancy, after invasion, was estimated to be 2 weeks.

The Headquarters of 203 was the secluded Coleshill House at Highworth, near Swindon, Wiltshire. Training included unarmed combat, using explosives, setting booby traps, standing still for hours and moving silently. Annual Patrol Competitions between winning Patrols from the 201, 202 and 203rd Battalions were held, and Icklesham Patrol twice represented Sussex. They won in 1942, each member receiving a tankard, and came second in 1943.

The Sussex H.Q. was Tottington Manor at Small Dole in West

Sussex. Also based here were 2 Scout Patrols, East and West, who helped to organise and train the Auxiliary Units in their area. Lieutenant W.Ashby led the East Sussex Scout Patrol, which was made up of 13 men from the Royal Sussex Regiment. In February 1943 they left to return to their Regiments and from then one Scout Patrol covered all Sussex, led by Lieutenant R.Bradford. The East Sussex Scout Patrol had at least 2 hideouts, one being in Beauport Park at Hastings.

By 1941 the County had 134 men in 21 Patrols. The men were chosen for their detailed knowledge of the local countryside and their personal qualities. East Sussex had 14 units - and Icklesham and Iden were in the Rye area. There were four on Romney Marsh: Mushroom Patrol at Snargate; Truffle Patrol near New Romney; Toadstool Patrol inland of Dymchurch and one at Lydd. Each Unit had it's hidden underground hiding place- or Operational Base (O.B.). These special units were stood down on November 30th 1944.

THE ICKLESHAM PATROL:

Mr Colin Cooke's Memories: Interview in 2001.

I was born in Udimore in 1917. I was in the Home Guard in the war, and they thought it would be a good idea to have a Secret Resistance. They picked 6 of us for the The Icklesham Patrol. Jack Merricks was Patrol Leader and other members were Dick Merricks, Alan Cooke, Colin Cooke, Don Cooke and Jack Jones. Five of us were cousins and all were involved in farming. We were nearly a family. People did not realise what was going on - not even our parents knew about it.

Our patrol area was Udimore to Hastings and back to Winchelsea. Our 'Hideout', or 'O.B.', was in a wood by a sand pit - down the road before the Robin Hood, from Icklesham to Pett. The Royal Engineers built it, as we worked such long hours on the farms. It was made of corrugated iron and timber and was 15 feet by 10 feet, and just over 6 feet high. The entrance was through a hatch, counterbalanced, which was covered with twigs and leaves. We then went down a shaft by a wooden ladder. There was a 15 feet long wooden emergency tunnel exit to the edge of the sandpit. Inside the hideaway were triple bunks, food for about three weeks, water in milk churns, ammunition, explosives, a small stove for cooking and a chemical toilet.

We went to Coleshill House, Highworth, near Swindon and Tottington Manor at Small Dole in West Sussex for instruction. I also remember going to Huntley, near Aberdeen, for three days training. This included flying over an area and then landing and carrying out all sorts of tasks using the information we got from the aerial views.

We spent long hours training and we stayed many times in the hideout. We were not supposed to stand up and fight, there were only six of us, but we were meant to slow the Germans down, with things like trip wires attached to explosives and 'flesh-cutters'. We were to sabotage what we could. The Army taught us shooting and we could have done quite a lot of damage by blowing up munitions, bridges, railway lines and such like. We aimed to patrol at night and to snipe at them. We were also meant to get information back [to the Resistance HQ.]. There's still a trip wire in a wood at Beckley. There's a plaque in commemoration of us put there. We did exercises against the local Army Headquarters. We would break into the house, and leave or move things, to say we had been there - on the bedside table and so on. The next time we went into the Unit we would say 'You were broken into.' 'No we weren't' and then we could prove it. They could all have been blown up if we'd laid a bomb!!

It was exciting at times and it took up all our spare time, after long hours spent on the farm. It stopped in the last year of the War when the Germans were busy fighting the Russians.

Mr Jack Merricks farmed on the family farms at Icklesham. On the first day of its formation, he joined the Rye Unit of the Home Guard (then known as the Local Defence Volunteers). When the secret underground movement was organised, he was made leader of the local group, was twice mentioned in dispatches and awarded the B.E.M.

THE IDEN PATROL

Mr Frank Reeve's Memories: Interview 2001

It was about 1940, when there was talk of imminent invasion and things not going well, when somebody decided to form these suicide squads. We were in the normal Home Guard originally, in the evenings and weekends, for work had to be done in the day. A captain came one afternoon into our store, the one we used for grading apples, to see me. (I can't remember his name, but I can remember hearing that he was killed in the desert later.) He was a regular army officer who was obviously told by somebody to come and start this group. It was called the Iden Group but it was nothing to do with Iden, it should have been called the Peasmarsh Patrol.

He possibly started the Icklesham one too, because we were pretty close together. We were never allowed to know about them. We didn't even know that Jack Merricks was leader of the Icklesham Unit. It was kept pretty secret. I was living with my parents, and doing farm work, aged about 17. My parents weren't supposed to know anything about it, but they must have known what was going on. We didn't talk about it. I had to swear an oath, I didn't sign anything, but they took my word for it. When I came home after the war there wasn't any mention of the group. Like a lot of things it died!

Soldiers came down to Peasmarsh; everybody knew something was going on because they put up "Danger Mines" signs, and then after a week or two the soldiers just disappeared. It's [The Operational Base.] still there, but the roof has collapsed; you can still see the escape route. It was only a Nissen hut buried, camouflaged and constructed by [Royal] Engineers. There were bunks, cooking arrangements, toilet, (an old Elsan thing), supplies, and ammunition. I never stayed overnight, thank God; it was as damp as hell in there, with no heating. We all turned up one day here in my father's breakfast room, and we took a vote on who would lead, and John Winter got the vote. We chose him because of his character; he was just an ordinary farmer, from a well-known family round here. We thought he would be the best man to follow. There were 5 of us. I left about 1943 to go into the air force so I don't know what happened after that.

The aim was to try and obstruct; to be a nuisance while it lasted; to be a nucleus for resistance when people got over the initial shock. We had quite a lot of training; we became quite proficient. It was exciting and I had no fear, well you don't at that age. They used to bring sections of railway line and we had to bend them, putting bits of explosives on either side; and we used to go and have shooting lessons and so on. We mostly used Playden Wood for the training. It was very isolated up there and don't forget Peasmarsh was just a small place; now its half a city! There was nobody anywhere near really. There was the old keeper's cottage near the top of Church Hill, there was Clayton's Farm, there was 'here', and the pub.

At the oast by Iden Lock, Raydon's Oast, which used to belong to John Winter, and at Saltbarn, we used to go and practice shooting with 2 rifles. And then we went to the ranges and so on at Coleshill. We wore uniforms and looked just like ordinary soldiers; they took the Home Guard insignia off the shoulder.

MR JACK MATTHEWS MEMORIES

Interview by T.P.C.C. Local History Students in 1990

Iden Patrol had six members, there was John Winter, of Saltbarn Farm, Playden, Patrol Leader; me, Jack Matthews of Leasam Farm; Frank Reeve of Lea Farm; Jack Goodwin, owner of an agricultural engineering firm at Rye; Walter Dawes, farm worker, and Bill Bailey, commercial artist of Beckley. Frank Reeve was eventually called up. Our formal training in combat skills, explosives etc. was at Coleshill in Wiltshire and Tottington, and we met to practice three or four times week - with tree stumps and old rabbit warrens! We didn't stay overnight in our HQ.

Our hideout (O.B.) was in Norland Wood, 500 yards east of Peasmarsh Church. The Royal Engineers built it, as it was a difficult site by a steep slope and a stream. Like an underground Nissan hut, its entrance was like Icklesham's, I'm told, and it had a phone line to it.

You pulled a hidden cable which allowed a wooden hatch, with about four inches of soil and grass on it, to rise a little - so that you could get your fingers under to lift it; this let the counterbalance work to lift the cover. The emergency exit was a concrete tunnel about 30 feet long and 2 ft. 8 in wide, which ended on the stream bank. Another wooden hatch, covered in soil, hid this. The hideout contained similar equipment to the Icklesham one. We had scores of grenades and spare detonators; hurricane lamps; picks and shovels; numerous rolls each of tripwire and trapwire (they were different!); a lot of pull and release switches; all kinds of ammunition; 10 gallons of paraffin; a large amount of plastic high explosive; many 1 hour and 3 hour delay switches for booby traps; lots of striker boards and magnets; hundreds of time pencils; 'sticky' bombs to put on armoured vehicles and black, brown and green camouflage colours to put on our hands and faces. Each of us had a small, very sharp, hook shaped knife to cut tyres. The first aid kits had morphine to use as a pain killer, or in a large dose, for suicide. There was also a gallon jar of rum!

My kit was the uniform, a pistol, ammunition, rubber truncheon, camouflage veil, fighting knife, steel helmet and I had a knuckleduster. John Winter, the Patrol Leader, kept more stuff at his house like rifles, an American Thompson machine gun, which fired 800 rounds a minute, and 4 British Sten guns, with magazines for them.

Mr Matthews described the sabotage methods practiced and said that the targets would have been things like the railway line at Rye and the A 259 and A 268 roads to Ashford and London from the town. He told of a meeting where an Officer asked for volunteers willing to be dropped into France before the Normandy landings - all volunteered but were not called.

Miss Penny Pattison told of a Secret Bunker in Moorbred Wood near the Hermitage.

Women and Girls in War

SHEILA MILLER; AUDREY HATTER;
JOAN SHERWOOD

Rye was a Garrison Town during WW2. Residents were very much a minority group as many young families were evacuated. For those who remained life was far from dull - much coming and going of Armed Forces of all nationalities. Social life was very fulfilling; dances every night held either at the Monastery, the George Hotel, the Drill Hall (now the Fire Station), even at the Methodist Chapel. Often there were dances at two separate venues on the same night. There was no shortage of dancing partners for us females!! We had a great War!!

We dare not venture out without our Identity Cards. One of the Guard Posts was on Monkbretton Bridge. During the day the Military would ask to see our Cards, but at night we were subjected to the whole ritual of "Who goes there? Friend or foe?" etc.

We were fortunate as we were not targeted for bombing raids, but were on the receiving end of 'Hit and Run' attacks and the odd bomb or landmine jettisoned by a returning bomber. Life became quite hazardous when the flying bombs ('Doodlebugs') started. These were continuous - you lost count of the huge numbers.

All 'large' houses were requisitioned for billeting the forces. The Freda Gardham School became a 'Stone frigate' - H.M.S.Haig. Several private houses backing onto the School were taken over as a sickbay and W.R.N.S quarters. The ratings were housed in Nissan Huts built alongside the Camber footpath. The Royal Navy also used the Camber Tram for transport to the coast. The shore establishment was used as an invasion staging post involving the use of Tank Landing Craft.

MRS CECILIE PREBBLE (nee Vigor)

The first thing that I remember about the War was in 1939, when I was 3, and we moved into Kings Avenue, Rye from the farm where I was born, at Starlock, Military Road.

For a few years I really didn't know what was going on. I can remember having our milk delivered by my uncle; my mother would put out a bowl with a plate on it. If I got a chance I would skim off the cream; the times I got told off for doing this!!

I started school with my sisters when I was 5. We had to go over by the Railway Station and we had to have a gas mask at all times. I didn't like putting on mine, and I still don't like anything over my face.

When they evacuated the children, my sister Dorothy, 7 1/2, and I were sent away to Blackwood in Wales and we hated it. It was a very dirty place, not green fields like we had left behind. There was not much food and we had a bath in a big tin tub in front of the fire. The W.C. was at the bottom of the garden and the house was filthy. The lady took our clothes and sold them, and when my mother sent any money, she kept it.

On returning from Wales, my father seemed to be always going out at night. We didn't know where he was going. Much later it turned out he had to ride his bike to Lydd Army Camp to be on duty each night. He had no lights on his bike and the road was full of potholes.

The Navy was at the top of our road, now the Freda Gardham School, and the Army was all around. It seemed that all day long big lorries and tanks were going through Rye; lots also came on trains. I shall never forget the parties the Navy fellows gave us children, and going out to see the Army men on the railway bridge with the big guns.

We couldn't go very far from home in those days at all, but I remember we all were very happy children.

DORIS SCOTCHER (nee Carey)

In 1942 I became an Accountancy Assistant for Rye Borough Council at the Mermaid; the main Hotel was empty. Captain Dawes, Town Clerk, interviewed me and I did general figure-work in what is the

Tudor Room for H.J. Wood, the Finance Officer. The Council was being audited at the time; in those days the Mayor appointed the Auditors. Later our office moved from the Mermaid to the High Street.

I accompanied Mr Wood arranging homes for soldiers etc; he was the Billetting Officer. Several times I was an escort on an East Kent Bus to Staplecross with child evacuees to/from the Railway Station, on holiday from Bedford. Throughout the War, I also took the men's wages from the Office, through The Needles, to the Cyprus Place Depot to pay them.

There were dances nearly every night - Molly and I would cycle up the Harbour Road (Father was the Chemical Works Manager), across the Lock, and leave our bikes in the Cottage there.

In 1942 was the Bombing of Cinema. My brother Bill, on Army leave from Iceland, was walking past with my mother. They were put on a bench outside Jones Garage (Central Garage) as dead. The Vicar came and said, "Who is this? I think they are alive." They were taken to Rye Hospital before transferring to Pembury, where Guy's Specialists were working. Bill received chest injuries and my mother had cement in her face and lost two toes. Nobby Clarke, who ran the Queen's Head, rang Mr Wood to tell me what had happened. I didn't recognise her.

MRS ROSALIE ELDRID (nee Green)

I was evacuated with Rye Grammar School to Bedford. My mother used to lend a room to Mr A.R.Jacobs, Headmaster, so that he could interview parents of each year's new intake of pupils who would go to Bedford. The first Christmas holiday when we came back to Rye, a 'Restricted area', we didn't need Identity Cards, but on all subsequent occasions they were checked at the Station.

The Royal Artillery camped in Mason's field behind our house on Udimore Road, where the playground now is. They had huge wheel cheeses and we used to exchange sardines, which mother had in the-larder, for cheese! (Our ration was tiny!) Mother had some of the soldier's wives staying with her.

The sentries on the old Ferry Road Bridge told us about Dunkirk and warned us about an invasion.

Mr Blackman, Senior School Headmaster, and St Mary's Church Warden, who lived at the bottom of Cadborough Hill, stored rations of tea, biscuits, powdered egg, flour and soap etc, for Cadborough, in case the bridge was blown. We kept chickens in the garden; we relinquished our one egg a week ration, to get feed. We also fed them vegetable peelings etc. We grew vegetables in the front garden; carrots, beetroot and onions - onions were like gold dust!!

We were in 'Bomb Alley' in 1944; 'doodlebugs' sounded like a motorcycle going uphill and I watched them when home for the summer holidays. I recall one: I saw the light in the tail before the engine cut out over what is now Badger Gate. The flash was seen before the explosion and it came down near Marley, killing a horse.

Rosalie gave us a cutting from the 'Sussex Express and Herald' of March 29 1945 about her father and brother: "When Flying Officer J.L.Green of Rye touched down on a Palestine airfield the other day after a flight from England, he found he was only three miles from his father's camp. Phones rang and contacts were made, and soon Flying Officer Green and C.Q.M.S. T.L.Green were shaking hands after a parting that had lasted nearly four years.

The official permit authorising the meeting said 'Make it snappy,' but the maternal streak in Dame Nature intervened, and she sent a sandstorm to delay the take-off for another day and a night." Mrs Eldrid told us that the meeting was near Tel Aviv and that they were both wearing pilot's wings - "my father's from the First World War when he was in the Royal Flying Corps."

BETTY PAINE (nee Cutting)

I remember I was about 5 and my sister was 2 1/2. My father was on Home Guard duty at the time and we came out of the pantry after a raid. My mother, sister and I stood in the sitting room to see we had no roof to our house and, there on the floor, was chamber pot that had fallen down from the bedroom; it was still in one piece except for a crack.

My Mother had a broken wrist; my sister was very badly shocked and I had been hit with shrapnel. I still have the marks today.

We had to stay with my grandmother in Tyneside until they re-housed us in 58 Ferry Road. We were given £50 to furnish our house, as we had lost everything.

In the new house, we spent more time in the Anderson shelter in the garden, than in the house! A bomb dropped over the back of our house and, on coming out of the shelter, we had to dig ourselves up to the back door. We seemed to have everyone's garden dirt in ours!!

Shops at the Landgate before the War

Maurice Blackman
Memories of a child - 1938-45

The day that war broke out, Sunday 3rd September 1940 at 11 am, I was playing on my own on the Cricket Salts and the siren started to wail. I was no stranger to the sound because in 1938 the Civil Defence and the Red Cross, in conjunction with the Town Council had organised an exercise to test the local rescue services. The siren had sounded then, so we Ryer's were quite familiar with the noise.

For the purpose of the exercise the houses that stood on the now Bedford Place car park, which were condemned, were ideal. We children and adults were bandaged and labelled describing our injuries and put in the rooms of the houses. We were then rescued, carried out to an ambulance, and taken to Rye Hospital where we were given tea and biscuits and eventually sent home. We kids thought this great fun.

Little did we know that during the next six years this would be all for real. At that time I lived in the Public House, called the Bedford Arms, which was the family home from early 1937 until my mother retired in 1958, so you could say we were in the Front Line. I could write a book about the goings on in this establishment during the War, but that is another story.

However, after the declaration of War things were fairly quiet; Rye had its quota of London evacuees.

During and after the Dunkirk evacuation, things started to move along. Pillboxes were built adjacent to Monkbretton Road Bridge and the Iron Railway Bridge, and a line of fortifications was dug between the bridges along the riverbank. As a child, I helped the troops to fill the sandbags required for the trenches. Heady stuff for a youngster! Incidentally the pillboxes still stand today. I often wonder if they would have stood up to a German bombardment if we had been invaded. The Cricket Salts had barbed wire entanglements across them.

The Battle of Britain with the Hurricanes and Spitfires battling overhead during that hot summer of 1940 was exciting. I remember the

Rye Radar Station being attacked one Sunday. We watched it all happening - the whole area was covered in smoke and dust. We thought the Radar masts would surely be destroyed, but come the evening, the dust cleared and they were still standing. We kids gave a great cheer!! During the Battle of Britain I remember we used to shelter under the arches of the road bridge that spanned the railway adjacent to Bridge Place. These arches became quite a community centre with families in the area being allocated an arch. We took tables, chairs, bunks etc. and spent many a long day and night under the arches. A man called Horace Hatter used to stand by the door of our arch and gave a running commentary of what was happening overhead. Of course, during this time we missed a lot of school, but we didn't mind - it was all very exciting.

As time went by, the defences at Camber were put in place, such as they were. You were restricted to where you could travel. The Monkbretton Bridge and Iron Railway Bridge were mined, so they could be blown up in the event of invasion. I remember there used to be a curfew - I remember I was stuck in Kings Avenue one night - and there I had to stay. My mother was not very happy. I stayed with Clive Pope for the night.

All through the summer, while the Battle of Britain raged, quite a few troops arrived in our area. Consider we were on the Front Line and, if the Germans landed, they would be needed. As kids we used to march behind the troops with our Woolworth's tin hats and our kit - the gas mask was a large Oxo tin, carefully covered in brown paper and stuck with tape. Our ammunition pouches were the small oblong Oxo tins - also covered in brown paper. As you can imagine, these tins became very scarce and if you had a full set you were the 'Sergeant' of our gang. Cricket stumps and manufactured wooden daggers were our rifles and bayonets, and as I had a full set of cricket stumps, I was able to supply our gang with sets of weapons. I could go on and on about all the things that we used to do.

We now come to the evacuation of Rye in July 1940. The film showing at the Cinema was 'Wizard of Oz' with Judy Garland. We went to see this and, when we came out, our mums were waiting for us, as there was an invasion scare (Operation Sea Lion). The Town Clerk told us that Rye had to be evacuated very quickly. Rye children were sent to Bedford and Somerset. They had their gas masks, a small case, sandwiches and a label tied to their lapels to identify them and were sent off by train from Rye Station to the various destinations allotted to them.

Margaret, my wife, who was six years old at the time, and her nine-year-old brother Tony, were among them. As Tony was told by his mother not to be separated from his sister, they were the last to be billeted, as no one wanted two children. After a long journey and being separated from their parents, you can imagine how frightened they were.

As for myself, I was evacuated to my Grandmother in Horsham. I went by taxi driven by Mr Bannister, who had served in the First World War, and who was employed by Bryan's Garage (now Skinners). I took with me my No 5 Set of Meccano, my toy soldiers and fort, my teddy bear and various other toys. I suppose I was one of the lucky ones with all the gear I was allowed to take. Being billeted with my Grandparents probably sounds great. Grandma was a Victorian lady in ways and dress and I was expected to wear Victorian clothes. The situation was not all honey! The water was pumped from outside and life was quite Spartan. Horsham was quite an active place in the war.
I only had one Christmas away from Rye - as I returned in late summer 1941, to be bombed out and machine-gunned coming out of School!

Monkbretton Bridge today

The Recollections of Clifford Bloomfield

Prior to moving house in 1936/37 to New Road, my mother had supplemented the housekeeping by giving bed and breakfast to touring cyclists. My mother graduated in 1937 to taking in longer stay people, such as temporary office, shop and building workers, and, as the threat of war progressed, she next took in men engaged in war preparations, building the town's air raid shelters etc.

Others constructed the then secret Radar Station at Brookland. The site of this was 600 metres beyond the Kent Ditch Corner on the A259. During 1938 one could see the growing pylons clearly from Rye. They stood in a direct line with New Road, looking east. Eventually there were 4 of timber construction standing in a square, each 75m tall, and 3 made of steel. These stood in a line, each 112m tall. When passing them fairly closely on the A259, one could see that the spaces between them were festooned with aerials. Rumour in Rye at this time was rife - stories of secret rays that would be capable of stopping the engines of approaching aircraft etc.

After the construction men had left, technicians arrived. I remember the little silver AMES badges in their lapels. The letters stood for Air Ministry Experimental Section. Finally, uniformed RAF personnel were billeted with us. Three came to begin with, all only just having joined the service, and then a further three, who slept in the house of a single old lady at No. 31. Mother provided them with their daily needs at our house. It worked quite well as they worked a shift system. What days!

Mr Tim Healey was one of these airmen, who, after the war, married one of my sisters - history repeats itself, as my other married a billeted soldier in the First World War!

1939 : FIRST SCHOOL AIR RAID DRILL.

This was probably in the early spring. I imagine, looking back, the school administrators must have been seriously contemplating the problem of the safety of children in the event of an air-raid. On one particular afternoon the fire bell rang for a fire drill. We assembled in the playground in our respective classes. A roll call was taken and then the headmaster informed us that an air-raid drill would now take place and the school premises were to be evacuated. We formed a long crocodile and were led across the fields in the direction of East Guldeford, some 600 metres distant, to a dry ditch. We were directed to lie down within its banks. After a short while we were re-formed into the crocodile and returned to resume school.

In retrospect, and in the light of air-raid experiences, what a target 200 children would have been, strung out across the open fields! Later 4 surface type air-raid shelters were built during the summer holidays in the school field.

On September 3rd 1939 people, including Ryers, tuned into their radio sets waiting to hear if our country was to be at war with Germany. Our Prime Minister, Neville Chamberlain, had set a time limit; if by 11 am he had not received an answer from the German Government that they would withdraw their troups from Poland, then this country would be at war. No reply was received.

I remember walking with my sister across the town to my grandparents. Whilst there, the air-raid warning sounded: it turned out to be a false alarm. But it frightened a lot of people at the time.

AUTUMN 1939 : Proper air raid drills were now carried out by quickly filing into the shelters. One boy having gone home to tell his mother of these exercises, was told that the next time they had one, he was to cycle home immediately, as she considered it safer to have him with her in the event of a real air-raid. In fact he actually did this on the next exercise.

CONVOYS OF REQUISITIONED VEHICLES

At this time I had noticed many small convoys of requisitioned commercial vehicles, (including buses), travelling westwards along the A259. They had obviously been quickly painted in camouflage - khaki. These vehicles were probably being used as a stop gap until war factories could produce purpose built vehicles.

SOME MEMORIES OF LOCAL WAR PREPARATIONS

There was much activity by the Local Authority directed by the Government. My father attended evening classes on Civil Defence. These included Gas Warfare, which was taken very seriously by everyone - very much in the way that Nuclear Warfare taxed our minds in the Cold War.

TRAINING HOUSES. These were a terrace of old Coastguard Cottages, which had recently been condemned as unfit for human habitation and whose occupants had probably been rehoused in Kings Avenue. They were much like those at Camber and were known as Lucknow Place. They stood parallel to Fishmarket Road on the site of the Car Park next to the Bowling Green.

I remember being taken, as a member of a party of schoolchildren, to one house. It was fitted out as a show house to demonstrate the way in which the public could take precautions against air-raids and gas attacks. All its windows were covered in strips of crisscrossed sticky paper to lessen the shatter of flying glass caused by bomb blasts. It showed black curtain material or boards which could be put up in the windows at dusk. The entrance doors had to be hung on the inside with a blanket, so that no light might show outside during blackout hours.

Fire- fighting materials included a bucket of sand and one of water, and a stirrup pump to tackle the small incendiary fire bombs that might come through the roof, or land in the garden.

Cupboards were to be stored with all kinds of tinned food and I remember eggs in a bucket of isinglass solution to preserve them.

One room was to be set aside in an attempt to make it gas proof. The doors had a blanket hung over them with additional strips covering the door and window crevices. These were to be dampened in the event of a gas attack. The chimney received the same treatment and it was suggested that the safest place within the house was under the stairs.

Another house was equipped to train units of the Civil Defence, i.e. the Air-Raid Wardens and the rescue parties, fire-watchers, the Fire-Service, Ambulance and Police. One room in this house was set aside to give gas mask experience - the trainees had to pass through a room filled with tear gas.

AIR-RAID WARDENS. This branch of the Civil Defence was training for these duties during this period in 1939. In reality, with a small town like ours, premeditated air raids never took place, so that their role of walking the streets, warning by blowing a whistle, probably never happened, except during the worst days of the Battle of Britain. Fire-watching was also done. Many employers of larger establishments in the town had rota systems throughout the War for the staff, who were required to spend nights at their place of work in case bombs might fall. I acted as a stand in, spending nights at 16 Udimore Road, the Catchment Board Office, after 1942.

The then Borough Surveyor, Mr A. Cornner, was the Chief Defence Controller for Rye. His office was at 107 High Street, now the Art Gallery's Easton Rooms. Its frontage was heavily sandbagged to the top of the window facia board. When passing, it was necessary to walk in the road. as the bags took up all the pavement space.

THE CIVIL DEFENCE AMBULANCE was garaged at Bryan's Corner, adjacent to the Cricket Salts. Only the wall exists today. Mrs Hartley, who was the local GP's wife, was in charge of it.

THE DEMOLITION PARTY'S DEPOTS were at the Council Yard in Cyprus Place and the Bonding Stores in Wish Ward.

There is not a lot I can write about the LOCAL DEFENCE VOLUNTEERS / HOME GUARD. I do remember watching with interest as these men, with LDV bands on their sleeves, trained on the river bank and later, as the Home Guard, having action exercises with the Regular Army at weekends. As young boys we noticed that their rifles were not the army pattern Lee Enfield 303, but, I believe, a Canadian pattern. The Bridge Place Studio of Mr R. Curd of South Undercliff, used by Mr Perugini as an Arts and Craft Studio, was a Home Guard Commando Post for a short while.

THE POLICE FORCE was reinforced by volunteer Special Constabulary - the men, as today, being recruited from the population.

During the following years, I remember, on many occasions during the blackout, that two 'Specials' ; Mr Tom Upton and Mr Murrell, could be found sheltering from the elements within the recess of Victoria Lodge, Bedford Place. Its front door has now been brought forward from its original position. The telephone call box also stood here, making it a good shelter and a handy contact point.

THE TOWN FIRE - ENGINE was in their new fire-station adjacent to the Crown Inn, Ferry Road, and there was also the A.F.S. - the Auxiliary Fire Service. Later it became the N.F.S. - the National Fire Service.

A FOOD OFFICE was set up to operate the Food Rationing Scheme, issuing Ration Books etc., in the then unoccupied shop, now Strand Antiques. Next it was moved to premises on the opposite corner, at the bottom of Mermaid Street and subsequently to 17 West Street, to a house known as Santa Maria.

GAS MASKS. I remember one evening, early in 1939, when some local officials or Civil Defence people called at our house to fit the family with respirators or gas masks. We had a choice of small, medium or large, and our requirements were delivered sometime later in little stiff card boxes with string threaded through them for carrying purposes.

When war was declared everyone had to carry their gas masks, but very soon the boxes disintegrated, they could not put up with the wear and tear, especially by school children. It soon became possible to purchase various types of carrying cases, some were made of a stiffened oilcloth with a press stud flap, but we children generally had a simple tin cylinder into which the mask could be easily slipped - it was fitted with a cap and a plastic sling. After the fear of invasion passed the habit of carrying them faded. Only service men and women continued to carry theirs until the end of hostilities.

IDENTITY CARDS. Once again early in 1939, officials called at each dwelling with, I suppose, the aid of the Electoral Roll, to register everyone for an Identity Card. A personal numbered code was given, and to this day everyone in my family generation can recite it. My family code was EJMA 75 - then each member living at the house at that time was given an individual number. Head of the household, Father - 1, Mother - 2, my number was 4, so my code was EJMA 75 - 4. My eldest sister was not then living with us, so she was given a number appropriate to her address. I note in Mr Cutting's Memories, he gives his number as EJMC - 224 -1.

BLACKOUT ARRANGEMENTS.

BUILDINGS. When War was declared in 1939, there was a great rush to buy black out material to cover the windows, mostly black cloth and thick black paper. People scoured the shops. I went with my father to Thos. Hinds, Timber Merchants, at the Strand (now the site of Strand Court), to buy a sheet of thin plywood, rationed to one per customer. We took it home and cut it to fit our 2 m x 1.5 m living room window. A pair of timber blocks were screwed to the edges so that it could be picked up to put it into the window recess easily. Not long after, I decided to paint - on the inside of the wood, a night sky of very dark navy blue, a yellow moon and pin points of yellow for stars. This served for our living room blackout throughout the War, being put up at dusk and taken down every morning.

VEHICLES. For vehicles driving at night it was extremely difficult, but one became accustomed to the conditions. All private vehicles carried a 5cm wide continuous white border to the front and back and along the lower edge of their sides. The head lamps were masked by a fitting which looked like a miniature top hat over the face of the lamp with three horizontal slots to allow a small amount of light to escape, not to light the way, I think, but so as to be seen by other road users.

Military vehicles lights were also masked, but at the rear a small white light was directed onto the white painted differential of the axle, completely hidden from above.

In the early days of the War, we saw the first white lines in the centre of the roads. A man would use a wooden frame, a pot of paint and a brush - all done by hand! I would think he was continually wearing out his brushes!

SIRENS. From 1939, the town's air raid warning system consisted of a wailing electric siren before an impending air raid, saying that enemy aircraft were in the vicinity. The siren would sound a rising and falling single note, lasting for probably a couple of minutes, whereas the 'all clear' was just a single steady note of equal duration. The sirens were positioned thus :- the original one at the Fire Station, Ferry Road for the town generally and, from October 1943, another was put on the Landgate Tower for the eastern side, and a third on the Winchelsea Road Martello Tower for the western side.

By day, initially, these warnings were taken seriously, but, with experience, as nothing usually happened, they became accepted with just a little apprehension. At night, however, it could be a little disconcerting, when aircraft could often be heard and we didn't know whether they were ours or not! It was often said, and believed especially by the older people, that one could tell German planes by the uneven drone of their engines: pure fantasy!

In fact, during a period in 1942, German FW190 fighter bombers would fly in from the coast very low, drop a bomb, cannon and machine gun the neighbourhood and be gone before there was time to give a warning!

PUBLIC AIR RAID SHELTERS EARLY IN 1939. Communal shelters in Rye were of the surface type, constructed on a concrete base of reinforced brickwork or concrete blocks. They had a flat concrete roof with an L- shaped blast wall to protect the entrance door at one end. Officially they were known as Fly Shelters. Sites that I remember were - 2 on the Town Salts; 1 at the rear of the Bedford Arms; Cyprus Place; Crown Field in what was Ellis Bros. Yard; Military Road near the Globe Inn; in the car park at the Ypres Castle; in both yards of Lion Street School; in the yard of the old Mermaid Street Boys' School; 2 in Mill Road near the Territorial Drill Hall (now the Fire Station); 1 near the site of the public phone box at the bottom of Mermaid Street; 2 in the Pipemaker's Arms car park; another in a cul-de-sac off Cadborough Road, (now Udimore Road); at least 2 in the Monastery in Conduit Hill and 1 in Wish Street. The exterior of the last one is still in existence, having been converted into the base of a dwelling known as The Shelter. The 3 schools had their own shelters - 4 at the Senior and Junior Schools - and these were made available to the public after the children had been evacuated during the Battle of Britain - August and September 1940.

At the base of the Gun Garden Bank in South Undercliff, opposite to Alsford's Timber Warehouse, there remains a brick blast wall. This was built to cover the entrances to some Anderson steel shelters, partly buried into the bank. Their primary use was for the staff of the East Kent Bus Depot, my father included.

The railway had 2 underground shelters, for railway personnel - 1 immediately east of the station building and the other in Budgen's car park.

At the rear of the row of shops in Cinque Ports Street, opposite to the Post Office, an access door was cut for a private underground shelter through the Town Wall - it still exists. Langton's Vaults, now Adams, was also a shelter. Although it was private property, it was made available to the public, with its entrance in Conduit Hill or High Street.

During 1940/1 private air-raid shelters were supplied by the Government through the local Council, who, I believe, erected them. They were known as Anderson shelters and were set about 1 metre into the ground. Made of corrugated steel sections, with an arched roof, they had ends of the same material. One end had a rectangle cut out for entry. The floor was sometimes of concrete, otherwise of earth and they were fitted with 4 wooden slatted bunk frames. They were banked up on either side with local earth and they could hold 4-6 people. They were supplied, I think, to people who did not have close access to the larger public shelters. I remember a number in Landgate Square, but they mushroomed from every available small patch of open ground near dwellings.

5) STATIC WATER SUPPLY. On many open sites throughout the town, many static water supply tanks were erected from 1939. All of fabricated steel sections, there were 2 types - a circular one of about 13m in diameter, with 2m high sides - and a rectangular type with var-

ious dimensions to suit their particular sites. Circular types stood on the corner of the present bowling green and on the open site of 18 Cadborough Cliff. Rectangular ones were in the Ypres Tower car park, on the bomb site adjacent to 45 the Mint, at 2 Mermaid Street, at the Strand Quay end of the Pipemaker's car park, and another on the smaller look-out at Hilders Cliff.

RAILINGS FOR SCRAP METAL. Almost all of the terraced house developments of the Victorian and Edwardian periods had small front gardens surrounded by cast iron ornamental railings or fencing, as did many individual properties. All was to change in the early months of the War as gangs arrived with oxyacetaline cutting equipment and removed all of them, except those areas where they served as guard rails. Places such as Hilder's Cliff, the gates at the rear edge of the pavement at either side of the Baptist Chapel and in Cinque Ports Street, where they guard a steep step down, were examples of these. In fact one set of garden railings did survive - they were probably overlooked - at Eagle House. Mr and Mrs A. Newton, an Aunt and Uncle of mine, lived there from 1939-65.

All this scrap metal was collected in the Railway Goods Yard and loaded into wagons and taken away to be melted down. One can still find the cut off stubs on many of the garden walls.

MAGNETIC MINE PONTOONS: H. J. Phillips Boatyard, Rock Channel.

Visiting my Grandparents home in late 1939, I found my Grandfather, who was then 75 years old, sorting out and cleaning his shipwright's tools. He was to return to work for Mr Bert Phillips in his Rock Channel Boatyard, where he was to show a gang of men the way to caulk the seams of a number of timber pontoons which they were building for the Admiralty. The material used was hemp and Stockholm tar - this was hammered in using special caulking irons.The pontoons were approximately 12m long by 3m wide and were to be towed by Royal Navy mine sweepers for the detection of magnetic sea mines. About 6 were constructed.

EVACUATION TO RYE

1939-40 : During the first months of the War, many scholars of the Lewisham Roan School arrived in the town. It was a bit short sighted of the authorities to send children nearer to the Continental coastline than away from it! They left the town around the Dunkirk period.

A BAD WINTER JANUARY 1940

This winter was particularly bad - the deepest snow that I have ever seen or experienced. I had been feeding the Y.F.C. animals over the Christmas Holidays, but once the snow had fallen, school was not resumed for some time - at least a month. To walk across the field to the hens and ducks in their arcs was a knee deep exercise. It was decided to erect a shed in the playground and leave the poultry inside. I believe at this time it was decided to wind up the school farm, selling off the stock and the buildings.

The R.A.F. men living with us worked shift periods, being taken daily by R.A.F. transport to Brookland. On the first day of snow they had to walk, and then they spent many hours clearing drifts before they were able to resume their normal journey. We children spent many hours and days on Leasam Bank sledging down the footpath area to Rovendene Cottage. One particular morning, when at the top of the Bank, on looking into the small copse of trees there, we discovered a great mass of leaflets strewn amongst the trees. They consisted of sheets of German Food Ration Coupons, dropped at night by a British aircraft returning from a leaflet raid on Germany. At that point of the of the war, it was a very common exercise to bomb the enemy with propaganda leaflets; the reason was, I suppose, to interfere with the enemy's rationing system.

OUR FIRST AIR-RAID SHELTER

SPRING 1940. 13 YEARS OLD: At this time my father decided that he would construct an air-raid shelter in the garden for our family, based on his experiences of World War 1 and its trench warfare.

He convinced us all that the safest place was in the ground, so he and I set about digging a trench in the far end of our garden, about 3m long by 1m wide by 2m deep. At this time he had heard of some thick hardwood boards being washed ashore at Camber, so, over a period of some evenings, we cycled to Camber, collected a few boards, tied them to the pedals and frame of the bicycles and then pushed them home. These were then placed over the trench and covered with earth, leaving an entrance at one end. We cut steps in the ground for access.

To me this was great fun, now that the schools had closed. Little did I realise the gravity of the situation, for I was to spend many hours sitting there, on the shelter, watching the aerial battles, which became daily occurrences, very high in the bright blue sky of that summer. The aircraft left great white tangles of vapour trails to record for a short time the battles that were occurring overhead. This was my most vivid memory of the Battle of Britain. Occasionally aircraft were seen crashing to the ground - a Hurricane towards Camber Castle, a Spitfire beyond East Guldeford and also the odd white parachute quietly floating to the ground.

I remember one particular occasion when aircraft were high in the sky. My sister and I were at the shelter when we spotted the old lady over the garden fence next door but one from us, sitting under her cherry tree with a metal dustbin lid on her head. We watched in great delight and noticed that she had a small cushion supporting it with a belt buckled under her chin, her hands clasped to the rim, looking apprehensively to the sky!

EVACUATION FROM RYE

The Rye Schools, having returned after Christmas Holidays and the heavy, prolonged snow falls of January 1940, continued air raid shelter drills and, in the late spring, we had an epidemic of cabbage white butterflies. The school organised a competition to see who could collect the most dead ones. They had to be brought to school in jam jars, and, my goodness, didn't they smell! All this was in response to the "Dig for Victory" campaign on radio, cinema and on poster, and was our effort to save the cabbages! One little thing about the poster puzzled me - it was a left-footed person pushing the spade in the ground!

(The mention of jam jars, as common throw away receptacles, gives a hint of a changing life style. Cooked teas were then very rare and jam and bread for tea was more usual.)

The new Ferry Road Mixed Primary School was, I think, opened for only one term, when, as with the other Rye Schools, it was closed in July for evacuation. The children of parents that consented to have their children taken, were billeted with families in villages to the south of Bedford - the Grammar School was in Bedford town itself.

During August the Authorities made it possible for Mothers, children and old people to evacuate. Those that decided to leave were placed with families in the West Country, Somerset mostly, but some went to South Wales. The majority of people returned after the Battle of Britain and the threat of invasion had passed.

THE SPITFIRE INCIDENT : APRIL 1940

Early one evening, I watched a Spitfire circle the Camber Fields, and to my utter astonishment, it landed in a field bordering the Camber Road, near the Broadwater bend.

Next day at school it was a great talking point, as we could see it from the first floor windows. After tea I quickly left our house to take a closer look, crossing the fields, to find two soldiers guarding it - its squadron code was RN-U.

About two days later, whilst at school, we heard the aircraft start up, and after some revving of its engine; it took off, circled and then disappeared.

A sequel to this event occurred in the summer of 1987, Through the "Rye Gazette", I learned that an ex - RAF pilot had been making enquiries. He wished to find out if anyone in the town remembered the event. I contacted Mary Owen to pass on the information just described, and to say, if it was the Spitfire concerned, the field was still owned by Mr H. Catt of Folley Wall, East Guldeford. Mr Catt eventually met the pilot on the site and the farmer recalled how he had taken up some fencing to give the pilot a longer take off path.

THE A.Q.C. OFFICE.

1940 ONWARDS. Throughout the war period, the town was always a garrison for various military units. They were accommodated in the many houses which were unoccupied, especially in the town centre - Watchbell Street, Mermaid Street. Houses on the outskirts were used too - Saltcote, Point Hill, Mountsfield, Woodrising, Fairladies, and Leasam House. For some unknown reason the then empty Lion Street School was not used by the Military - we used it twice a week for meetings of the Air Training Corps.

The A.Q.C. Office was to be found at No. 3 High Street - the letters, I believe, stood for Army Quartering Commandant. It took charge of requisitioning unoccupied properties for the garrisoning of troops, and of land for military purposes. Passes were issued to civilians having essential duties to perform in military restricted areas such as Camber and Winchelsea Beach - this included myself - mine had to be renewed monthly.

It was common practice, in the early days, for soldiers to come to our drawing office to make copies of large scale Ordnance Survey maps, in order to plot on them the many mine fields in the coastal areas.
After 1942 this office transferred to Saltcote Place which was now the local Military Headquarters. It was also a military contact office for the local population.

One particular house, the Hooks at Playden, was used by the Army throughout the duration of the war. I have known Mr Trevor Venner for many years - he is a true "Ryer". In his early days he lived in Ailsworth Lane, Landgate. He was called up to join the Army in 1939 and spent some time training with the Royal Artillery on Salisbury Plain. Posted next to Okehampton, Devon, he was attached to the

Devonshire Regiment, which formed part of the 45th Infantry Division. Where was he next posted to ? - Rye! From June to September 1940 his billet was "The Hooks".

Some weeks after moving in, in the summer of 1989, one fine evening the owner received a knock on the door. He found a man in his late 60s, who apologised for his presence, but he said he could not resist coming to the house where he had spent many happy times living with other men of the Manchester Regiment. He said he had left at the end of May 1944 and had then taken part in the D Day landings, losing many friends. He then asked if the shower was still there. The man explained that it hung in the rafters of the shed at the rear of the house. They went to the shed and there, in the rafters, was a large rusty army biscuit tint its base peppered with holes. He explained that one soldier would stand on a step ladder with a bucket of water, whilst the other took a shower It's still there 46 years later!

JACK NEWTON : MAY 1940

During the German offensive in 1940, when the British Forces were being driven back to the French coast, my cousin Jack Newton was captured in Boulogne. He was serving with the Royal Engineers and, like many captives at that time, was taken on long marches to West Prussia. He was in a prison camp called Stalag XXB.

On February 2nd 1943 he was shot in the camp by German guards and the reason was never made clear. My Aunt and Uncle received a letter which said he had been buried with full military honours and was buried in the village graveyard of Serbersdorf, Marienwerder, West Prussia.

DUNKIRK FISHING BOATS : MAY 1940

Two Rye fishing boats took part in the Dunkirk evacuation that I know of, the Dorothy Margaret and the Mizpah, although I believe the Mizpah was not a Rye boat at that time.

PREPARATIONS FOR THE DEFENCE OF RYE

ANTI INVASION MEASURES MIDSUMMER 1940.

After the invasion of Dunkirk, there was a period of intense activity in order to defend South East England. Rye, in particular, we now discover, was probably to bear the brunt of this attack, the flat marshes providing landing areas for enemy aircraft and the long shingle slopes of the sea shore line to take the invasion barges. Its date was set at September 15th 1940, but all this was unknown to us at this time.

Much civilian labour was drafted into the area to cut poles from local woodlands, each about 6 to 7m long and they were transported to the Marsh to be planted in all the fields considered capable of receiving landing aircraft. The poles were in a staggered pattern at roughly 50m apart. Other fields were protected with scaffold tube. "A" frames were set up on either side of long narrow fields, with a wire hawser suspended from frame to frame, anchored into the ground at each end. The fields between the New Road school and the river were treated in this way.

SEPT. 1ST 1940: Mr Arthur Court was, for many years, the General Foreman with the Rother and Jury's Gut, the then local land drainage authority. He lived at Scots Float House, Military Road, adjacent to the depot and was affectionately referred to as 'father' by the work force. During the war period, he was a special constable and when in social company would tell this story:- Driving back to his home from Wittersham on Sunday about 2pm, approaching the New Bridge over the Rother at Iden, he noticed a man standing beside the road. On approaching he seemed anxious for a lift. Stopping his car, Mr Court thought to himself that this was an airman. He asked for a lift in English, but Mr Court noticed a German accent and the realisation struck him. Out loud he exclaimed in surprise "A b....... German!" The man went on to say, "I believe I am on the road from Tenterden to Rye. I need treatment, having injured my hand and arm." Mr Court helped him into the car and started off to Rye Hospital. The German became quite talkative, saying how he had lived in Hastings prior to the war. His name was Burschgens. His aircraft had, in fact, made a forced landing and had collided with one of the numerous steel wire anti invasion measures previously described - the Messerschmidt 1O9 finishing up on its nose.

On this same Sunday lunchtime another ME 109 crashed very close to Strand Bridge, Winchelsea.

ON THE SEA SHORE, a vast length of scaffold tubing barrier was constructed from Cliff End, Pett Level to Dungeness and beyond. It stood at about medium tide level. The Rye Harbour entrance was left open, but provision was made to block it with large floating logs linked together with wire hawsers.

SETTING THE SEA ALIGHT. At the entrance to Broomhill Farm near Camber, another bizarre scheme was devised to set the sea alight. Great tanks of fuel were set into the rear of the sea wall road embankment. Concrete bunkers to contain pumping equipment were built and pipes passed under the road and through the sea shore. The idea was that, on the approach of enemy landing craft, the pumps would fuel the sea and its surface would be ignited with mortar flares. This burning fuel operation was actually tested and for many years after the event, the timber groynes remained charred and the beach stones above high water had turned pink and white due to the high temperatures created.

All reference to town and village place names were obliterated or removed from shop fronts, posters, vehicles, etc. An example can still be seen in Market Road on a stone of the Rye Literary Club. The engraving had been filled in with cement mortar, most of which has been removed since, but traces still remain. All highway sign posts were removed. It probably did not cause too much of a problem to a traveller because there was so little civilian traffic, other than bus services and local deliveries. I cannot think that any of these measures would have hindered an invading army.

I remember witnessing all the small boats within the harbour and river being collected together and being taken through the Tillingham Sluice. They were then tethered together between the sluice and the railway bridge awaiting their mass destruction in the event of invasion. Many remained there for the duration of the war - some simply breaking up through neglect.

Thinking back, the town of Rye must have been allocated 2 anti-aircraft guns which arrived almost as soon as the schools evacuated. They were 40 mm Bofors guns - one sited across the playing field of the Senior School from our house - now the site of the swimming pool. The second one was in Rye Harbour Road, now the site of the Jehovah's Witness meeting house. As these sites became permanent for the duration, they had buildings of prefabricated concrete alongside them, which were the living facilities for the gun crews.

From time to time other guns of this calibre would appear and be set up on other sites around the town, but only for short periods - such as at the rear of Badger Gate, the Gun Garden, a site beyond the last house on New Winchelsea Road known as "Half Moon Battery" (a name from the Napoleonic era), and also at Leasam Farm. Doubtless there were others that I was unaware of.

SEARCHLIGHTS. The nearest to Rye was opposite Offens Farm, East Guldeford, on the A259, mid way between the Star Crossing and Kent Ditch Corner. There were many more in the locality, as could be witnessed at night, when they so often combed the sky - more in practice than in defensive action.

THE BRITISH ARMY were generally made up of regiments or units with a distinctive cap badge. But they were also absorbed into larger formations such as divisions, corps, commands -- so that one would find a number of different regiments in one formation. The formations were distinguished by a cloth shoulder patch on uniforms and their vehicles carried the same insignia both front and back, so that they became very familiar in the town. Men of the anti aircraft and searchlight units were of the Royal Artillery, but their formation insignia was of the Anti Aircraft Command - a red square depicting a black bow and arrow held by a pair of fists. From 1940, there was to be a military presence in our town until the war's end and this included units of all three services. I have already referred to the RAF and their activities.

The Royal Sussex Regiment, Irish Fusiliers, and some units of the Devonshire Regiment, (a detachment of the of the 45th division), were also stationed in the area manning artillery positions. Their Division sign was of Drake's Drum.

There were also units of the Royal Artillery stationed in and around the town, before and through the period of the Battle of Britain. The role of defending the town in the event of invasion was theirs, but once this threat had ceased, they left us to be replaced by others. Thinking back, my memories of the early period are a little hazy, but I can confidently name the groups. From mid 1940 the troops took on a training role for the events to come, when our troops would return to Europe once again.

Rye's immediate natural defences were the River Rother on the East side, Rock Channel on the South and the River Tillingham on the West, Each of the bridges crossing these lines were charged with explosives and guarded day and night.

PILLBOXES . The railway bridge over the Rother had a concrete pillbox to defend it on the town side, which is still in existence today. Monkbretton Bridge's pillbox was close by the Fishmarket and it was demolished in 1970. The timber board walk of the footbridge was removed for the duration, so that all pedestrians had to use the road. A pillbox was situated on the headland between the River Rother and Rock Channel - removed in the 1960's. Another, in Phillip's Boatyard, Rock Channel is still in existence, as is the one at Brede Sluice, by the Sluice Keeper's Cottage on Rye Harbour Road. The Tillingham Bridge and Sluice crossing was defended by an underground bunker. The site is under the brick paved area by the traffic sign to the right of the Strand Cafe. Its gun ports were at road level and camouflaged as a grassy knoll. The Mill railway bridge and Ferry Road bridges had no defending pillboxes.

At the time of the construction of these pillboxes and many others around the countryside, they were camouflaged by using sections of timber holiday buildings taken from Camber and Winchelsea Beach, as timber sheds and the like. (All the population of Camber and Winchelsea Beach had been forced to move out leaving ghost villages, occupied by military personnel only).

To close the defensive ring around the town, the northern side, from the River Tillingham at Rovendene Cottage a chain of concrete dragon's teeth were constructed in four alternate rows as a barrier, stretching up Leasam Bank to a point between Hill House and the Ambulance Station on the A268, where an example remains. It recommenced on the wide grass verge on the east side of the road and turned into the present garden of Shellfield. (Here a section lies buried.) It follows the south side of New England Lane, down to the Cliff Edge overlooking Military Road. It recommenced on the east side of Military Road to terminate on the bank of the River Rother.

Two further sets of Dragon's Teeth were set in the river bank at the rear of 109 Military Road and also in Deadmans Lane which could be blocked by them. Two still exist there behind the railing fence.

The A268 and Military Road openings through the system were to be closed by a concrete block barricade, the blocks being stored at the road edge until required.

The design of the blocks was quite ingenious. There were two types of concrete blocks. One was pear shaped with a rounded base, each stone having a central hole through it, where a steel bar was to be inserted. Each block would be linked together by a steel chain set across the road. The idea was that if and when a vehicle attempted to push through the blocks, they would gyrate and roll erratically to snare vehicles. Defending troops would then put the vehicle out of action and thus increase the block by its presence.

The second type was a cylindrical block able to be rolled into the road and be stood on end with the aid of a steel bar. This would create a solid obstacle in the same manner. Both types of road blocks are still to he found, usually as road verge bollards.

Within this defence perimeter were batteries of 25 pounder field guns on two sites.

One was in Tillingham Avenue, just beyond the last of the terraced houses. These guns were set in a steel ring on concrete etc. bases and could be traversed to cover the northern approaches to the town. An avenue of high elm trees existed along the path at that time and made good cover. I remember the guns, limbers* and vehicles were all covered by large camouflage nets supported on posts. There were probably three guns and their bases remain to this day.

(*A limber is a trailer used to carry the guns' ancillary equipment and ammunition, and which, when the gun is being towed, goes between the gun and vehicle.)

The second battery of 25 pounder guns were to be found in the small field at the rear of houses 51-63 South Undercliff facing south. They were also under camouflage nets. The old Scout Hut served as a billet and cookhouse - a bungalow called the Anchorage and Mr Paine's bungalow on Shipyard Lane now stand on its site. A number of Howitzers were sited to the rear of the Rother Iron Works. These guns covered the sea and approaches to Rye Harbour.

Outside this defensive ring were many other concrete pillboxes and a 25 pound artillery position on the Camber Road, opposite the Rye end of the Golf Links.

A battery of heavy artillery was sited in the wood adjacent to the entrance of Fagg Farm (now known as Gillshaw Farm), at the top of Udimore hill, and was manned by troops from Newfoundland.

Their formation insignia was of the XII Corps - it was raised in Kent and Sussex for the purpose of the counter invasion. The insignia depicts three native trees - the oak, the ash and the thorn.

These heavy guns were well placed to cover Rye Bay and the marshes.

Those of us still living in in New Road / Kings Avenue, found ourselves now outside of the town's perimeter defences. Each time we wished to cross over Monkbretton Bridge, day or night, we would be stopped by the sentries - men of the Irish Fusilliers who had just returned from the Dunkirk evacuation. After a week or so, the majority of us were allowed to pass unhindered as we became known.

At night it was quite a different situation, for on approaching the bridge in the darkness of the blackout, we knew that at any moment a sentry would call "Halt! Who goes there?" We would reply "Friend!"; His reply was "Advance friend and be recognised!" It was then a case of showing our Identity Card or it was taken from us, so that we would be required to repeat our Identity Number correctly. Then the timber and barbed wire barricade was drawn aside and we were allowed to pass.

The ensuing weeks saw many modifications to the Monkbretton Bridge defences. Great concrete square blocks were built on either side of the road with slots which allowed steel rails to be passed through; concreted slots in the road surface were made in which tall, large section stanchions bent at 60º angles, could be implanted in the roadway; and walking over the bridge, we accepted the sight of the menacing wires running along the bridge structure to the explosive charges.

To this day there are concrete cylindrical blocks, as described, still remaining at the rear edge of the footpath, by the fresh fish shop.

Going back beyond the 1930's, as many of my older contemporaries will recall, it was common practice to go for Sunday afternoon walks in the town and surrounding countryside, dressed in our "Sunday Best". I know we generally did, and often my Grandparents came too. During the early and mid 1940's, one or two of the RAF boys would join us. They were ordered to carry a rifle and a respirator at all times, and I remember, as a 13 year old, eagerly carrying the rifle for some part of the way. Can you imagine being in company with a service man carrying a rifle in Rye today?

BICYCLES : MAY 1940

A register of all bicycles was prepared by either the Local Defence Volunteers or the Police. [*P.C.Moppett was one who did this in Rye. Ed.*] They visited every household, shop etc. and noted the frame number and a general description - using a chart. In the event of an enemy landing, these cycles were to be gathered in, either to be used by our own forces or to be destroyed.

KING GEORGE VI's VISIT

During the counter invasion preparations, I remember about mid-summer, King George VI visited Rye and lunched at the George Hotel. He inspected our defences.

TANKS IN RYE

1940: Fair Meadow, Rye Hill, at that time was like open parkland and a good number of mature oak trees were spread over it. I recall seeing, when on our Sunday afternoon walks, a tented army camp with vehicles and tanks standing under the trees.

LATE 1941. A large number, probably about 20, Waltzing Matilda medium tanks arrived at Rye Station by train. I watched them being unloaded into the Station Approach. Once they were all assembled, they moved off. I think the whole town turned out to see them. They went along Cinque Ports Street, Tower Street, Landgate and then turned into Bridge Place to cross the railway line across sleepers, as the bridge could not take their weight. They continued up Rye Hill and that was the last I saw of them.

1943: Convoys of military vehicles passing through were almost a daily occurrence, but this time they were accompanied by a large number of heavy Churchill tanks. They too passed through Cinque Ports Street, Tower Street, and Landgate, but, at Deacon's Corner, they turned into Bedford Place, These ungainly vehicles were rather unpredictable when rounding the bend on the tarmac road. A number of them clipped the concrete kerbs along the frontage of the Bedford Arms. The evidence is still there.

One of these tanks probably broke down soon after leaving Rye in the A259, for within a couple of days, a tank transporter, with tank, returned, retracing the original route of the tanks. But, when it was time to turn from Landgate into Tower Street, the driver changed his mind and tried to take it through the Landgate Tower, where it became

lodged. It was freed by letting the air out of the transporter's tyres. The tank's name was "Sawdust".
1943-44: Frequent convoys were accompanied by tanks and armoured cars, generally, at this time, American -Stewart's and Sherman's.

BOMBING OF THE RADAR STATION: AUGUST 12TH 1940

On this morning, I had just crossed Monkbretton Bridge on my way home, when, looking down the long straight of New Road, two aircraft were flying very low towards me. As they came to the houses, they lifted and banked away to sea. They were a couple of Messerschmidt M.E.110's. It was about 10 o'clock.

During the afternoon I was in our back garden when I heard distant explosions. Climbing onto and standing on the rear fence, I could see smoke rising from the Radar Station and aircraft weaving abut the sky. We awaited the return of the RAF men at tea time, when they arrived with stories of the action. The black smoke was caused by bombs bursting in the vehicle park. We were led to believe that there was no other serious damage - a comment I remember was that the height of the pylons and their mass of aerials had prevented the diving planes getting near their target. It has been said by various locals that the aircraft were Junkers 87 Stuka Dive bombers, but this was not so. The aircraft that appeared briefly in the morning were on reconnaissance and were the same type of aircraft as in the afternoon raid. This raid on the Brookland Radar Station was the only one made on the station during the War. The RAF personnel were transferred soon after to their newly constructed camp at Brookland - the present Phillipine Village.

OUR FIRST EXPERIENCE OF THE BATTLE OF BRITAIN

As I remember the beginning of the Battle of Britain, and it must have been soon after the Radar Station was bombed, we were all sitting at tea when the steady sound of aircraft could be heard. We quickly went outside to watch, very high in the sky, little silver aircraft, some making vapour trails. There were dozens of them, all in formation, flying inland. We were very curious about the "unknown" vapour trails; it was the first time we had seen the phenomenon.

RYE'S FIRST BOMBS : AUGUST 18TH 1940

It was on a Sunday lunchtime that bombs were dropped on Rye for the first time. German bombers were returning back from a raid and, as I watched them from the entrance of the garden shelter, they flew low over the town. I did not see the bombs drop, but the line of the stick can easily be traced today - if one starts at Godfrey's Row (now the Council's lock up garages); then to the Mint - two bombs exploded front and back on the open site adjacent to No. 47 which had been a dwelling and also the Police Inspector's office at one time, Francis Sinden and his family were bombed out there. The next hit was across the road to the rear and side of Faraday House; then No, 2 Mermaid Street and finally the Garden Room of Lamb House which was demolished.

Other bombs, dropped this day, landed in the area of the Old Brickyard and Udimore Road. People killed were Mr G.Bumstead, Mrs F.Bumstead and Mr J.H.Bumstead.

MOVE TO THE SCHOOL SHELTERS : AUGUST I - SEPTEMBER 1940

Finally the pressure of this daily activity broke our resolve to use our shelter and we joined the few remaining residents of our part of the town by going direct into the Senior School surface shelters when we heard the siren. In our case, it only required a climb over the garden fence. Personally I disliked these shelters - being herded together in the dark. There was no mains electricity but a large battery type lamp at one end. People were talking constantly - it somehow revived the spirit of hop picking, families bringing their food and drink, some with bedding etc., but I always wanted to watch the events going on outside.

A DAY DURING THE BATTLE OF BRITAIN

On this eventful day, September 11th 1940 in the afternoon, we were once again sheltering in the school surface shelter, when rifle fire was heard outside, above the roar of aircraft. Some of the older men opened the door, and I, ignoring my Mother, just had to see for myself. There, coming very low over the school and the shelter, was a Heinkel III German bomber. It was gliding with spluttering engines, going in the direction of Camber. This was one of a number of such aircraft that the soldiers in the school playing field, had been and were firing at, that afternoon. These men of the Irish Fusiliers were extremely excited!

Since writing this item, I have received a snapshot taken on that very day, (with a box camera), by a soldier serving on a field gun battery at Gorse Cottage near the Golf Links. He took it standing at the bedroom window looking East. Using features and angles, I believe the Heinkel III, described above, crash landed south east of Moneypenny House, in an area known as Sisley Land. I recall there was a pause as it went from view and then a great pall of black smoke rose from the site.

A second Heinkel III crashed and burned out at Chittenden Cottage, an isolated farm dwelling NE of Camber. Thirteen miles away to the NE at Burmarsh a third Heinkel crashed and burned. Two Hawker Hurricane fighters also came down, one burned at New Romney and a second at Scotney House, midway between Jury's Gap and Lydd. All these aircraft crashed between 4 and 4.30 pm on a bright clear afternoon.

After the "All Clear", we climbed back over the school fence into our garden and into the house for tea. During these later weeks of the Battle of Britain, the RAF men had left us to live in their new camp at Brookland.

Our latest lodger was an Army Intelligence Corps Officer. He used a military motor cycle, which was not only useful for daily personal transport, but it proved its worth when crossing fields to crashed German aircraft. His duties, I understand, were to interrogate German prisoners of war. During the evening of this day (September 15th), he told us that he had ridden out across the fields to the bomber we had seen crashing in the afternoon. In fact it had pancaked intact, but as he approached, he saw the crew setting it on fire.

OUR EVACUATION : SEPTEMBER 12th 1940

The very evening of the 11th September 1940, after the day's events, my Father returned home from work and he and my Mother decided that we would evacuate. The danger was becoming too much to bear. The Intelligence Officer was told he would have to find alternative accommodation straight away and by 9 o'clock the next morning, my Mother, three sisters and I were on the train to Bedford. Passing through Ham Street Halt, the train hardly moving, we saw a crashed Heinkel 111 bomber beside the railway line. Arriving in the London suburbs, the train was constantly crawling along and stopping; finally, after being diverted, we arrived at High Holborn Station whereas we should have been in London Bridge-Charing Cross - no doubt due to bombing. The sky, I recall, was filled with barrage balloons. After crossing London by taxi, we eventually arrived in Bedford, and went to Kempstone, a suburb of Bedford by another taxi. We stayed with my Aunt and Uncle (he being my Father's brother from Cumberland). My Mother and youngest Sister stayed with them, my two elder Sisters were accommodated across the road and I, next door. I attended school in Kempstone and, although I did not know the district, I took on a paper round before school. I remember very clearly delivering papers on November 30th 1940, to discover that Winston Churchill's birthday was the same as mine.

Children were encouraged to collect acorns for pig feed at this time. I and others in our neighbourhood spent weekends in the local woodland doing this. It takes an awful lot of acorns to fill a one hundredweight sack! - and we did fill quite a few! I do not remember how much we were paid for them. Children there at this time had very noticeably brown stained hands, caused by breaking the outer husks from walnuts, which commonly grew in the district - I had never been familiar with this before.

I recall being awakened during the night by aircraft continually passing over the house and actually thinking they were German bombers.

The Strand and Strand House before bomb damage.

The Strand after an air raid, September 1942.

Battery House and Ypres Tower before war damage as seen from the Church Tower

Bomb damage to Methodist Chapel and Battery house, September 1942

Bomb damage to Ypres Tower, September 1942.

The Garden Room of Lamb House before 1939.

The remains of the Garden Room after the raid of august 1940. The piano belonged to E. F. Benson

This worried me very much and I spent the night down stairs. The family of that house were not bothered in the least, not having at that time experienced the activity of war. In the newspapers next day we read of the blitz on Coventry.

BACK TO RYE

Within the first week of December, Mother, my youngest Sister and I returned to Rye, having been away 2 1/2 months. My two elder Sisters remained working in a factory producing electric light bulbs.

The invasion threat had receded and the guards were taken off Monkbretton Bridge. During our absence, on October 3rd 1940, a stick of bombs had fallen across the eastern side of the town. The first demolished the rear of 31 Kings Avenue, craters from the bombs continued across the river, the Cricket Salts and Bedford Place; hitting houses then empty as the people had been rehoused in Kings Avenue - it is now a Car Park). The last bomb exploded at the rear of the Newsagents at 21 Landgate - "Miss Horner's" - this was said to have been an "oil bomb" - whatever that was!

Obviously the German airmen did not stay to see the results of their bombs. Having missed their target, the iron railway bridge and line running into Rye Station, the exploding bombs fell 150m in a precise line parallel to the railway. But this did not deter the German news media and radio recording this event.

Every evening of the week the British people were able to tune into Lord Haw Haw, as he was known, to listen to his propaganda broadcasts from Germany. So many of his statements were wild to the extreme. Within a few nights of our return, we were awakened by a very loud explosion that shook the house - followed by an eerie silence with no aircraft noise whatsoever. In the morning, with time on my hands (no school!) With other children, we soon discovered that a large bomb had exploded in the field at the rear of No. 50 Kings Avenue, in fact opposite to No.31. Looking round the crater for shrapnel, we children quickly began to collect lengths of green cord and parachute material. It was then realised that a parachute mine had drifted down quietly during the night. This crater is still traceable.

CRASH OF THE WELLINGTON : 17th DECEMBER 1940

During this night, a British Wellington twin engined bomber crash landed in the field north of the iron railway bridge over the Rother, about 100m outside the Borough boundary. It was completely intact but for its bent propellers. The aircraft's landing gear was in its retracted position and this had caused it to slide across the field. Evidence exists to show that this aircraft was returning from a raid on Mannheim and, being low on fuel, the crew decided to make a crash landing in the dark at I o'clock in the morning. It came to rest some 400m from the nearest house in Kings Avenue.

It was eventually dismantled in large pieces and taken away by an RAF maintenance unit. Some of these men stayed with us, for Mother had become quite well known by the Police and RAF throughout the war - in fact we often had these men staying with us for short periods as they collected crashed aircraft. The Wellington, on its "Queen Mary trailer", stopped outside our house, whilst the RAF men collected their kit before leaving.

RAF purpose built trailers for carrying aircraft were affectionately known as "Queen Marys". They were 18m in length and the name was derived from the Cunard Liner - the world's largest ship at that time.

MY FIRST JOB : JANUARY 1941

Very soon after Christmas, in January 1941, when I was 14 years old, I took a Job at the Rye Post Office, then in the High Street, as a Telegram Boy. I was given an official arm band and a typically heavy red bicycle with 28 inch wheels. The saddle was let down to its lowest position as I was a short young lad.

Behind the Post Office counter was a small room with a desk, a chair, the important "daffodil" type telephone, a block of blank telegram forms and yellow envelopes.

Although I was required to be available at all times, I did spend some time in the sorting office. When the phone rang, I would go to the office, but I was not permitted to answer it - only the counter staff! The

message received was placed in a yellow envelope, sealed and given to me to put in the leather pouch on my belt. A large map on the wall showed various circled rings of distance from the Post Office and I was given a time allocated for the delivery and return, before I left.
It was quite commonplace to cycle to Udimore, Iden Lock, East Guldeford etc., going to military outposts - the gun sites around the RAF Radar Station at Brookland as an example. I earned 50p a week. Telephones in the 1940's were not the common means of communication that they are today - hence the use of telegrams.

LOCAL FISHING IN RYE BAY 1941 ONWARDS

Fishing for the local boats became very good as the larger trawlers of the North Sea ports were now very restricted in their movements. Their customary long fishing trips were abandoned, being prevented by enemy action and also many of the larger vessels were requisitioned by the Royal Navy as Mine Sweepers and Fleet Auxiliaries. The initial war period allowed the fish stocks to multiply.

The small inshore boats of the South East that operated off the beaches were now unable to do so, due to the steel anti invasion barriers that had been erected continuously along the coast, except for the cliff shores. The fishermen were also hampered by the activities of the Royal Navy in the remaining small ports such as Newhaven, Folkestone etc.

Rye represented an opportunity for these men to continue fishing, so that the Harbour was inundated by small inshore fishing boats of many registrations :- NN = Newhaven, SM = Shoreham and Brighton, FE = Folkestone, R = Ramsgate, RX = Rye and Hastings. These boats were permitted to go to sea only in daylight hours.

The fish became so plentiful that it was common knowledge that if the trawl net was left in the sea for too long a period, it would be extremely difficult to raise, due to its weight. The Mizpah on one occasion, brought into the Fishmarket 280 stun (stones) of gutted fish, plus the last trawl of the day was left in the water until the ship docked. This is 1.75 tons - today a boat of comparable size would be lucky to bring in 100 stun.

Large groups of the local townspeople would gather at the Fishmarket to await the returning boats. They were able to buy generous quantities of a variety of small fish from the catch - a sand bag full for 5p - flats such as plaice, dabs, skate (referred to as Maid Wing), Angle fish known as keddlemar, dog fish known as Robin Huss, cod, whiting, John Dories, mackerel, herring etc. In this respect, Rye people were able to supplement their food rations very considerably.

During early 1943, all the larger boats were now armed with 303 anti-aircraft Lewis machine guns. These probably gave the fisherman some feeling of confidence in being able to hit back, if it should be necessary.

Not only was it difficult to raise a trawl net from the sea due to plentiful fish supplies, there was another problem of war debris snarling the nets - the wreckage of countless aircraft etc. It was interesting to see the variety of war debris brought into the Harbour and Fishmarket - many types of jettisoned aircraft fuel tanks - some long egg shaped and others sledge-like. This latter kind was carried by Spitfire mk 1X's. There was no end of such wreckage laid out on the river banks. German Magnetic mine trolley's were another curiosity - made of wood, all screws were of aluminium and wheels of plastic. These were from German Naval units sowing the mines at sea. There were also an great variety of buoys. All this must have required many hours of net mending and costly replacements.

INCENDIARIES AT RYE HARBOUR

Early in 1941, I recall a Sunday when some friends and I cycled to the Chemical Works on the Rye Harbour Road. During the previous night probably a few hundred incendiary bombs had fallen over a wide area. Here and there were little piles of grey and white magnesium ash with the little metal fins lying to one side, still intact.

MY SECOND JOB : APRIL 1941

I left the Post Office after three months and took what I considered to be a better job with the then local land drainage authority. It had rather a long title - The Rother and Jury's Gut Catchment Board and its offices were at 2 High Street. The Board employed a work force of about 130 in the maintenance of watercourses, structures, sea defences (not military) - groynes, seawalls etc. An increasing number of these men were driving excavators, dredging out watercourses. Each driver had a mate whose job was to clear undergrowth and prepare for the machine, and then tidy up afterwards. He also worked as a relief driver. The fleet of machines at the outbreak of war was 12, by the end it was 34 and, over this period, roughly 95% of all waterways had been dredged - throughout the Walland Marsh as far as the Rhee Wall and in all the upland valleys - some for the first time ever! The exception was Pett Marsh proper as this was flooded with sea water as a counter invasion measure in June 1940. Key men were generally considered to be employed on essential war work therefore not liable to be called up for military service.

Many acres of farmland that were not considered to be producing the amount of food expected of them, were taken over by committees organised nationally by the Ministry of Agriculture, Fisheries and Food. In our area it was known as the East Sussex War Agricultural Committee. On this land, the Women's Land Army was much in evidence.

I was employed as a chain boy at 65p a week the job required me to work with a land surveyor. I held a levelling staff and called the measured distances read from a tap, generally across rivers and ditches, before and after land dredging, so as to measure the excavators' output. I travelled the local countryside as a passenger in private cars. This was classed as essential use and petrol coupons were provided, whereas almost all private cars were laid up for the duration.

The surveyors included Mr Les. G. Locke and a little later two women joined us - a Miss Nora Hales, now Mrs Lane-Howse of Beckley and a Miss D.V. Harding. They had been trained in the use of the dumpy level.

TROOP MOVEMEMTS : SOUTH STAFFORDSHIRES

Early in 1941 the South Staffordshire Regiment came to Rye. Their formation insignia depicted a Staffordshire coal tip and pit headgear, not known to me at that time. As with many such formations, the insignia tells its own story of the area in which it was raised. The regiment was part of the 59th Infantry Division. They remained with us for some months.

TROOP MOVEMENTS : THE CANADIANS

Later in 1941, they were replaced by the Canadians. The first were the Essex-Scottish Regiment of Canada. They stayed a while, but I remember very well on one Sunday evening, hearing a pipe band in the distance. It seemed to come from the town so off I set on my cycle and crossing Monkbretton Bridge, I could see this band making its way up Hilders Cliff. I eventually caught up with them and followed them down the Mint, along Wish Street, Cyprus Place, Ferry Road to Cinque Ports Street. They were the band of the next Canadian Regiment to come into the town - the Toronto-Scottish - and this was their way of introducing themselves.

All of my generation will recall how everyone who smoked, (and in those days the majority of men did at least), were smoking cheap, freely available Canadian cigarettes. "Sweet Caporal" was the most common but a menthol variety was not liked. Many American brands were smoked too. The Canadians were generally hard drinking men and the local pubs probably did well, that is when they had a good supply of beer in their cellars.

One night my Father, who was rather short in stature, and who always cycled to work and back via the Fishmarket, was returning home in the blackout. He was stopped by two drunken Canadians and an argument ensued between the soldiers as to who should have the cycle. My Father was momentarily left holding the cycle and, realising that they were fighting, he made his escape and rode off quickly in the darkness. The insignia of these Canadian Regiments was of the 2nd Canadian Division.

THE GHOST OF BREDE PLACE

I spent my time working with all three surveyors, but at one time with Miss Harding. My impression was that she was of private means and did not really need a job, but chose to do something she chose rather than something to which she was directed, as could happen in war time. We spent many an hour during her early weeks with us looking for a house to buy. She was looking for an olde worlde country house - and there was a big choice.

One particular day we had been to an excavator working in the Brede Valley. The driver suggested she took a look at Brede Place as he knew it was empty - I think now he spoke with his tongue in his cheek! Driving in its direction, we stopped to ask the way, and we were told we should first find Miss Claire Sheridan. We did not know it at the time, but she was a cousin of Winston Churchill. On entering her drive, we found the grounds full of all manner of carvings, idols and tall totem poles. Miss Harding was not a person to be put off and up to the front door she went. She said to Miss Sheridan, "I understand Brede Place is empty and do you think the owner would be interested in selling it?" Miss Sheridan laughed, "I should not think so - it's been the family home of the Frewen family for 200 years! But you're welcome to look it over. The Canadian Army has only just vacated it and if you look round the grounds you will find the gardener."

This we did - he was an old man, working on a ladder, clipping a yew tree. We told him of Miss Sheridan's permission and he went to the summer house to get the key. It was so large it had to be carried by the shank. The two of us walked up the steps to the front door which had a Gothic arch. We turned the key easily, pushed open the door, entered the hall and then wandered the corridors and rooms up and down stairs until we came to a lower room. On opening the door we saw it was a small chapel within the house. Taking a cursory look around we left, closing the door, and passed into a small hall with another flight of stairs. About to continue along another corridor, we both stopped for some unaccountable reason, looked back, and in the closed doorway a misty figure emerged. I looked in disbelief - we were both transfixed as it moved across the hall before us and ascended the stairs and went out of sight. We hurriedly left the house, locked the door, returned the key to the summer house and got into the car. It was only then and as we were leaving, that we were able to relax and exchange our experiences.

I have rarely mentioned this to anyone. I still don't think I believe in ghosts, or do I? I mentioned this to Mr Layton Frewen of Northiam and he said the precise location where we had seen the ghost was known to his family. Brede Place was seriously damaged by fire about thirty years ago - I wonder if the "ghost" is still there?

A.T.C.

As a teenager in late 1941, I joined the newly formed Air Training Corps. We met once a week in the Lion Street Schoolrooms, using the Library room for indoor drills and P.T., the upper room for lessons in many subjects such as "the theory of flight", basics of navigation, the Morse Code, aircraft recognition etc. Our commanding officer was Mr G.D.Bear. He had been a long serving Royal Navy Chief Petty Officer. In Rye we were formed as B Flight of 304 Squadron - other flights were at Hastings, St. Leonards and Battle. There must have been upwards of 30 boys attending, although our individual members were constantly changing as they came of age for call-up at 18 years. I remember two outings - a day each at Biggin Hill and West Malling.

We, in Rye, formed a drum and bugle band under the tuition of three keen ex army musicians - Charley "Omody" Buss, his brother Jack Buss and Teddy Howe. I think we turned in some very good playing in Military Church parades and I remember going to a Church Parade in Hastings for the whole squadron, marching from Warrior Square to St. Leonards West Marina Church of St. Saviours.

THE MANCHESTERS : NOW 15 YEARS OLD

END OF 1941: With the departing of the Canadian forces, it was now the turn of the Manchester Regiment - they stayed in Rye for about three months. Their insignia was the Red Rose of Lancaster and they served as part of the 55th West Lancashire Infantry Division. The complete rose was on their shoulder patches, but a symbolic rose, based on the Tudor Rose, was on their vehicles.

DURHAM LIGHT INFANTRY : MID 1942

Following the Manchesters were the Durham Light Infantry - how different they were in their bearing! They marched at a pace of 140 paces a minute and their drill fascinated the locals by its speed. Most servicemen wore their forage caps according to military regulations across the right side of the head, with the two front buttons directly over the line of the nose. The D.L.I., however, wore theirs fore and aft over the centre of the head - probably in order to keep them in place during their rapid drills.

On a number of summer afternoons their military band was to be found on the Cricket Salts, seated in a large circle, entertaining the local population. One man I recall excelled on the post horn. I feel certain that this regiment was not attached to any military formation or division at that time.

THE AMERICANS : JULY 1942

Returning home from work one afternoon on my cycle, I arrived at the gate to find four large, khaki green, wooden trunks stacked on the pavement. Not knowing what they were there for, I went inside to be confronted by two American Army Airforce officers. They had just arrived in England and came directly to our house to be billeted with us. My shyness at that time was dispelled as they chatted about their first impressions of England and the stories they had heard of how we were supposed to be starving on our meagre food rations. Mother laid the tea as usual. Astonishment came over their faces as they saw it, for we had a greenhouse full of tomatoes, eggs from our chickens and home made strawberry jam. At other times there was an abundance of vegetables from our allotment garden and fish from the local boats. We were fascinated to see them eat, using only a fork in the right hand

and another time we were aghast to see them eating bread and strawberry jam accompanied by tinned pilchards.

Whilst writing about food, a little job that I undertook each Sunday morning was to produce a little extra butter. Whenever the milk pan was boiled during the week, the top was taken off and put aside in a jar until Sunday. We had a little glass cream maker with a Bakelite top and pump action handle. Into this was put the weekly milk toppings. I would then spend probably an hour or so pumping this, pouring off the buttermilk, to leave a few extra ounces of butter.

The four trunks were eventually carried upstairs and hadn't they come prepared? Fruit that we hadn't seen for three years, oranges, limes, lemons and grapefruit, and, of course, coffee. Mother was shown how to make this - American style, with a pinch of salt always added.

Coffee in bean and ground form was not generally drunk, at least by the majority of working people - not only had it been expensive, but it was now unobtainable. The popular coffee that English people drank was a joke - a bottled liquid coffee extract with chicory known as "Camp" coffee - still obtainable today.

Why were these Americans with us? A new radar station was being constructed and commissioned at Wittersham, operated by RAF personnel. I suppose the Americans were acquainting themselves with the then secret equipment. Some of the buildings remain - on leaving Wittersham on the Tenterden road, they can be found on the left hand side.

These men stayed with us until just before Christmas. Mother subsequently received a food parcel from the USA sent by one of the men's relatives, as a thank you for looking after their son.

These are the only American servicemen that I know to have been billeted in Rye, although in 1943-44, frequent convoys of their vehicles and armour passed through the town.

AIRFIELDS OF THE 2nd TACTICAL AIR FORCE

Late in 1942, Hall & Co. was working a ballast quarry (now part of Castle Water), and an aggregate plant at Rye Harbour. Their lorries were transporting drainage beach for the Air Ministry to selected sites on the marsh. It was being used to form airfields by filling in the ditches with the beach - it allowed them to drain in a limited way. In order to move these large quantities of beach, more of the company's lorries were drafted into Rye and their drivers were billeted here. My Mother took in two men from South London.

On Saturdays and Sundays I travelled with these men to Newchurch, Midley (which is half way between Brookland and Lydd), and Honeychild Manor Farm at St. Mary's in the Marsh. Even at this time, dummy aircraft were sited on the fields, in order to deceive the enemy into believing that these airfields were already operational. It was hoped that they might waste their time and ammunition on them!

Their real role was to allow fighter and fighter-bomber aircraft to operate over northern France, assisting the Allied advances after the D Day landings. Newchurch was also to become the main operational base in the fight against the flying bomb - an unforeseen use in these early years.

THE WELSH REGIMENTS

LATE 1942: After the Durham Light Infantry came the South Wales Borderers and they were followed by the Welsh Regiment. This particular regiment was rather a novelty in as much as the men wore on their backs five braids of material shaped like a fan. This was symbolic of the fact that they were the last British regiment to wear a black greased pig tail of hair. The two regiments were of the 53rd Welsh Division The sign of a letter W with a base forming the bardic crown, was their insignia. They left in early 1943.

HIT AND RUN RAIDS : AUTUMN AND WINTER 1942

During this time the towns and villages of South East England were subjected to attacks by German Focke-Wolf 190 fighter bombers. They carried one 500lb bomb as well as being armed with machine guns and 20mm cannon. They were referred to as Hit and Run Raiders. To help combat this menace, units of the RAF Regiment were drafted to the town and surrounding countryside. They were equipped with their standard airfield defence systems - small armoured cars fitted with a pair of machine guns. Other guns were sited on high static positions. I remember it being said that one such site was at the rear of Durrant House in Market Street.

Rye's first attack occurred on a Wednesday morning at about 8 am - it was September 15th 1942. Two aircraft roared over the town from the east dropping their bombs. One fell in the rear of the Mermaid Inn, but, probably due to the plane's low altitude, the bomb did not get into a vertical position, but bounced, leaving its fins there and bursting in the air. The second bomb demolished two houses, including Mr Brown's butcher's shop to the right of the bottom of the Green Steps, in the Strand. This also damaged Strand House and other surrounding properties - many loosing windows and tiles. It is possible that these aircraft, coming over the coastline very low and flying at a speed of some 400 miles per hour, were intending to hit Strand Quay as civil engineering works had started in that area to enable landing craft to be moored, serviced and refuelled in preparation for the D Day landings. In those days this was referred to as the Second Front and some activities were diversionary, to fool the enemy away from similar measures going on in West Sussex, Hampshire, Dorset etc.

On September 16th the Rye fishing boat Mizpah was fishing in Rye Bay when it was attacked by a Focke Wolf 190 fighter/bomber. It machine gunned and shelled the little boat killing two of her crew, Mr Hollands and Mr Longley. The skipper, Mr Charlie Locke, was wounded and subsequently he received the British Empire Medal.

Many fisherman were reluctant to go to sea for some time - but time is a good healer, and fishing soon continued unabated.

There were in the town, at this time, indignant protests being voiced, especially at Council Meetings. The fact was that the town's only refuse collecting vehicle had been used to collect the two bodies of the fishermen killed in the attack on the Mizpah, and subsequently, used to take them to the town Mortuary in the Ypres Tower. Questions were "who authorised the use of this vehicle for this purpose?"

Maybe unknown to Councillors and townsfolk in general, it had been used on a number of occasions before to collect the bodies of seamen washed ashore, a number of soldiers killed in our own minefields on the coast, and airman of both nationalities.

The vehicle's body was of welded steel construction with sliding shutters closing over it and with a hinged tail gate. It was thus leak proof and could be easily washed out, not only for this purpose, but as was frequently done for its normal refuse collection duties.

The feelings being expressed locally however were that it was an insult to the fishermen's families.

On September 22nd, after returning to the Catchment Board Offices at 16 Udimore Road, and parking my cycle at the rear, suddenly there was the roar of aircraft and instantly, explosions. I saw two F.W.190 fighter bombers flying low across the western side of the town, but, in fact, there must have been three. They left behind palls of rising black smoke. It looked, from where I was standing, as though at least one bomb had fallen on the eastern side of town, and instantly I thought of home. Off I set on my cycle, along Ferry Road, through the railway goods yard and, arriving by the Electricity Showrooms, there before me, was a great pile of brick and concrete rubble across Cinque Ports Street, where the cinema had disintegrated. It had broken through the high wall into the garden (now the car park) by the town wall. The Cinque Ports Hotel was also in a sorry state; smoke and cordite filled the air.

I did not wait, turned and headed back towards South Undercliff. On arriving at the Ship Inn, again I was confronted by building rubble. I left my cycle, for to my surprise, the woman surveyor that I worked with, Miss D.V.Harding, was actually taking charge of the situation, attending the injured and dying, instructing people just as the first C.D. first aid parties were arriving. I have since discovered that my colleague had been a practising doctor in Australia. The casualties were not Rye people, but working parties sent to repair the previous weeks bomb damage. The bomb had fallen in almost the same location and the Strand House was now destroyed.

I eventually arrived home via the High Street, not knowing that a third bomb had devastated the Ypres Tower area. For many days after this raid, the roadside gutters to the east of the town collected the drifting flock filling of the cinema seats. It is possible that the bomb was intended for the Railway Station - the Cinema was only 100m away.

One could also imagine the bombs in the area around the Ypres Tower were aimed at the Rother Iron Works-Bus Depot - again only 100m away.

On October 7th 1942, Mrs E. Clark of 11 Kings Avenue was making one of her regular visits to her aunt, a Mrs Smith of Tram Road, Rye Harbour, when, at 2.15pm, a F.W.190 dropped a single bomb on the house. It demolished it and killed both occupants. I recall this incident as her son John was a teenage friend of mine during these times. In fact he was working on the top of Landgate Tower as an electrician's mate, installing the new air raid siren. Hearing a distant explosion, he looked from his vantage point, to see smoke rising from the site at Rye Harbour village.

THE BEAUFIGHTER INCIDENT : OCTOBER 21 1942

It was on a Wednesday afternoon that an aircraft was approaching Rye from the direction of Lydd. As it came clearly into view, the Rye guns opened fire on the approaching aircraft. The bursting anti aircraft shells seemed to have no effect as it continued to fly just south of the town. Approaching Winchelsea it must have taken a hit or two, for it banked and crashed into the ground near Winchelsea Station. I stood and watched this event, knowing that the aircraft was British. It was a Beaufighter, but was mistaken for a Junkers 88 bomber, as these aircraft were not dissimilar. The British plane had taken no evasive action and it was suggested after the incident that maybe the crew of two were badly injured or even dead, after an action on the other side of the Channel. The aircraft did not release any "vary" lights - a colour combination for the code of the day would have been the practice.

Immediately after the action, I ran across the school field to the Bofors gun. Its crew were cock a hoop with joy at having shot down this J.U.88, but a field telephone call confirmed that they had, in fact, shot down a British aircraft. The crew of two were found in the wreckage. Squadron records of this aircraft state that a Lt. Brown of AA Command was "lectured today" and also state that, by a sad coincidence," a pilot new to this Squadron, Sgt. Wright, was shot down and killed on a sector reconnaissance today". *[I believe this to be 'shot down by friendly fire'! Ed.]*

This aircraft, together with a Focke Wulf 190 German fighter bomber that had crashed at Castle Farm on 4.1.43, were collected by an RAF Maintenance Unit whose members were staying at our house.

SUNDAY DECEMBER 6TH 1942. Having just got up from my bed in a rear bedroom at about 8 am, I heard aircraft coming. Quickly looking out of the window, I saw two aircraft pass over the roof. They were F.W.190's flying straight to the town centre. Machine gun and cannon fire filled the air, but no bombs were dropped. I watched them bank away to the sea on the far side of the town. On this morning Mr W. Edwards was killed on the Ypres Tower steps leading from Fishmarket Road and Mr Benny Gamble and Frank "Ikie" Wright, of Wright and Pankhurst, were injured. The anti aircraft guns around Rye were not successful, but Rye's day was to come.

FRIDAY 15TH JANUARY 1943: At about 3.30pm in the afternoon, I was standing in a field on the south side of the Rother near Scots Float Sluice, holding a levelling staff for my colleague Mr L.G.Locke, who was bending over his dumpy level, when 1 heard aircraft approaching. They seemed to be low, but I could not see them. Then instantly looking towards the high, tree covered cliff of that part of Military Road, an aircraft appeared - a F.W.190. All within seconds, this was followed by four others in quick succession, one dropping a bomb. I remember seeing, in the next terrifying moments, the earth and smoke rise skywards from the cliff top. But now I was clutching at the grass on the ground, as machine gun and cannon fired at us, as they passed over and some bullets landed literally beside us. They were flying so low that I can remember turning my head sideways and seeing the pilot's head in one of the planes. The Sluice keeper's house near us had been damaged, but no one had been injured. But the aircraft were now sweeping on towards Rye and, above the noise of their engines, the cannon and machine guns could still be heard. In Rye Mrs C.Batchelor had just collected her children from the Primary School in Ferry Road. Near the railway crossing they were caught in the gunfire. Mrs Batchelor was hit by a bullet in the knee and it is believed the same bullet then entered the stomach of little Sheila, then five years old, (Sheila is now Mrs Chillingworth).

The 40mm Bofors AA guns were in action but, due to the low roof-topping altitude of the aircraft, it was said that at least two shells passed into the buildings of the Rother Iron Works.

Recorded evidence shows that on this day, as these aircraft were crossing the coast at Winchelsea Beach, one was shot down by gunners of the 230th Coast Battery there. It crashed into the sea and the pilot's body was washed ashore at Littlestone.

Over the following weekend, I walked the fields where we had been levelling, picking up the spent machine gun and cannon shell cartridges cases, so I know how close and lucky we had been.

After that experience I remember thinking what a coincidence that Les Locke and I had laid terrified in a field and escaped, when only three months before, his father had suffered a similar ordeal but with serious consequences.

THE WILTSHIRE REGIMENT : EARLY 1943

The next troops to arrive were the Wiltshire Regiment. It was part of the 43rd Infantry Division and its sign depicted the Wessex Dragon. This Division had the longest stay in Rye and later saw very bitter fighting in and around Caen in Normandy in 1944.

TEATIME BOMBS : FEBRUARY 10TH 1943

Late on a grey drizzly, winter afternoon, a Dornier twin engined German bomber flew in from the sea at Winchelsea Beach to Rye. Turning over the north west of the town, it dropped three bombs in a line; the first exploding in the kitchen garden of Rye Cottage, opposite 4 Tillingham Avenue; the second made a direct hit on the railway line at the end of present day Cyprus Place - my Grandparents lived in the terrace next to the line and their house was rendered uninhabitable; the third demolished a terrace of three houses at the Strand, known as Havelock Villas, and an adjoining building that had served as the Custom House. Mrs M.J.Barham (the sister of my Grandmother) was killed, Mrs Dunk was seriously injured and her lodger, Mr E.J.Castle, a relief manager at the Westminster Bank in the High Street, was killed. It is believed that he was outside the house, having just arrived for his tea time meal. Mrs G.Axell, at the other end of the terrace, was also killed. The site is now occupied by the river frontage of Strand Court.

At the time of this occurrence, I was crossing Monkbretton Bridge on my way home to tea. I saw the aircraft in the darkening sky, flying towards Camber Castle. Rye's anti-aircraft guns were firing in its direction, but the glowing tracer shells were falling short of their target as it disappeared in the mist.

OUR SECOND AIR RAID SHELTER : SUMMER 1943

The production of war supplies was probably becoming more plentiful at this time and we were offered an indoor Morrison table shelter, which my parents accepted. It duly arrived as a load of prefabricated steel sections. We put this together ourselves - four heavy corner posts, angle posts top and bottom on the four sides and a sheet of 3/16 steel plate for the top.

Woven steel spring laths were clipped into the base (on which to place bedding), and weld mesh netting was fitted to three sides, although a fourth could be used. This stood in our living room under the window, taking up much of the space, as it measured 2m long x 1 1/2m wide x 1m high. It was a very awkward, immovable piece of furniture to live with.

As a matter of interest, a corner post of one of these shelters exists to protect the corner of Flushing House, Market Street, with the junction of Church Square, from high sided vehicles.

WAR SAVINGS APPEALS

The first was a national appeal by Lord Beaverbrook, Minister for Aircraft Production, called the "Spitfire Fund". Organised to replace the losses of the Battle of Britain, some people paid for a whole Spitfire, but in Rye it was a savings drive for a whole week. My cousin, sister and I decided we would do our little bit; we collected children's books and opened a children's library. Loaning them at 1d each on Saturday mornings over some months through the winter, we raised just over £7.

In other years, an organising centre would be set up in an unoccupied shop, in aid of such appeals as War Weapons Week and Wings for Victory Week. During this latter appeal, Mrs M.H.Mackechnie produced a painting of the then recently damaged Ypres Tower with Spitfires overhead. A slogan read "Rye's Reply" and it stood in the centre of the window of Simon Milne Gifts, High Street. I produced the Spitfire made from scrap wood for Mrs Mackechnie to paint four of them into the scene - I still have it! Also on display were war souvenirs, shrapnel, pieces of crashed aircraft and weapons. It was this week also that local army units put on a display of artillery and vehicles on the Salts. We children were allowed to turn the crank handles to raise, lower and traverse Bofors AA guns. The most popular were the Bren Gun carriers' rides round the perimeter of the Salts, very flat, except for the rise and fall over the footpath, twice! The soldiers also set up, between the fisherman's huts and the river, a live display of trench mortars, firing their projectiles. They were landing - and exploding - on the river salting at Northpoint Outfall - a distance of 1000m to the south east!

BOMBING OF NORTHERN FRANCE : LATE '43-SUMMER '44

British Hawker Typhoon fighter bombers became daily visitors to Rye. Always coming from the west, they would fly down the River Rother and at Rye Harbour village they would line up within the two harbour training walls. Flying very low, when they reached Lime Kiln Cottage, they would release eight rockets at a time - aiming at a large bargelike target just off the river mouth. This was a practice range to simulate the attacks these aircraft were making in Northern France on railways and shipping. The Radio news bulletins would refer to these activities taking place daily. "Our aircraft today flew sorties over the Pas de Calais".

Also at this time the Allied air offensive was building up, for we realised that the air craft passing over Rye were preparing for the Second Front; but there was also a more sinister reason of which we were ignorant at that time, but we were to discover at a later date.

One would often witness the raids by the American heavy day bombers, four engined B17 Fortresses and B24 Liberators on their out going flights. They would be very high in the sky, surrounded by fighter escorts of P38 Lightnings and P47 Thunderbolts and sometimes PS 1 Mustangs, going to targets much further afield. There were occasions when these aircraft were seen returning.

6 SEPTEMBER 1943: A memorable afternoon, the B17 Fortresses were seen coming in from the sea fairly low as individual stragglers. Many were so shot to pieces that holes could be seen right through the wings and fuselages. They looked hardly able to fly. One pancaked into the then flooded Pett Level marshes, still covered by sea water and a relic of the anti invasion measures of 1940.

Another landed less than a mile away in the Pannel Marsh, between Winchelsea and Pett. This one blew up and burned. A third came down in a large field at Reading Street, just off the Appledore - Tenterden road. This machine was repaired and fitted with replacement engines. It then took off to return to its base. Generally these heavy bombers were of the 8th American Air Force.

There was a distinct period when, at about 8:30 am, I was either crossing Monkbretton Bridge or about to leave the house for work, when the noise of approaching aircraft could be heard coming from the North. Then suddenly, coming into view over Point Hill, were formations of medium twin engined bombers, B25 Mitchells, B26 Marauders and B34 Venturas. Their markings could be plainly seen, generally these were of the 9th American Air Force, but one was a separate formation of Venturas belonging to the Free Royal Dutch Air Force.

It was customary for the Americans to test their machine guns over the English Channel. At 8 am on June 7 1944, a formation of Marauders - American medium bombers - had left their base and were flying towards the coast. Inland, from Scots Float (Star Lock), Military Road, machine guns could be heard; they were a bit premature with their testing as it should have been over the sea! As the aircraft appeared, one of them was pouring out black smoke; it was on fire. It instantly dropped its bombs into a small field at the base of the Cliff and the River Rother by the Star Lock Pub and none of the bombs exploded. The aircraft carried on getting lower and lower until it crash landed in a field beyond Barn Farm, East Guldeford. The crew extinguished the fire and all managed to escape. This aircraft had been shot down by one of the others in its own formation. A bomb disposal team arrived and had great difficulty in locating the bombs which had gone down some 3m.

CRASH OF THE B24 LIBERATOR : 24 June 1944

On a very fine and quiet summer evening at about 7 pm, I was in New Road, by the open ground which is now the school bus park. I heard an aircraft approaching from the direction of Camber. It sounded as though it was in trouble. It came into view high over the school building and beginning to turn, for a better view, I ran to my faithful flat roofed shed to see this four engined B24 Liberator bomber making a large orbit. It continued to do this, but the circles became small and receded back towards Camber. Then suddenly five 'chutes appeared from the plane and instantly the plane cartwheeled out of the sky to crash in a field at Wall Farm, Jury's Gap. It hit the ground in a great ball of fire and black smoke. To this day small pieces of debris can be found on the site.

ADMIRALTY M.F.V's : C. MORRIS & Co. ROCK CHANNEL

The old Rock Channel Shipyard of G & T Smith was given a new lease of life, if only to be its last. A company by the name of C.Morris received contracts to build a number of Motor Fishing Vessels. Although they looked like fishing vessels, I doubt that this was their purpose. They were destined for the Far East and Pacific War. Their displacement was in the order of 120 tons. Two were completed before the end of hostilities and two remained unfinished on the slips for some time after.

At the launching of the first one in mid 1944, I pushed my Grandfather in a wheel chair from New Road. I was feeling quite excited to see this event, but Grandfather's conclusion was - "They're nothing like we used to build 'em!" In fact one of these Rye vessels was recently known to be afloat and working as a fishing trawler named "Trewarventh" - PZ 196. Her owners are Stevenson & Sons, Newlyn, Penzance.

A MILITARY CONVOY WITH A DIFFERENCE

During late 1943 I think, although military vehicle convoys on the roads were taken for granted as a daily occurrence, there was a difference. For some three days without a break, convoys were all going in one direction - east through Rye from Udimore Road to New Road. Many were Canadian and this I do remember, for I was seeing Divisional signs not seen before. There were many different British signs and also countless American vehicles. It was staggeringly endless - all day and all night long!

History now tells us that this was a hoax - this movement of Allied forces was to deceive the enemy spies, or their reconnaissance aircraft into believing that our build up of invasion forces was to be in the east - and not in the west around the Hampshire ports.

THE MANCHESTERS RETURN: Early 1944: now 17 years old

The Manchester Regiment returned to Rye and here I will record an event that I witnessed. Having spent the morning out at work and then returning back to Rother House (our office in Udimore Road), it became known that Field Marshall Montgomery was in town. Leaving the office on my cycle to go home for dinner, I learnt that Monty's military train was in the railway coal sidings at Rope Walk. I went to look and I found the train standing parallel to the Agricultural Hall (now the Arcade).

All seemed very quiet there, just a few guards standing around, so I decided to continue home through Eagle Road. Rounding Deacon's Corner into Bedford Place was a short military convoy. It slowly turned into New Road and then took a sharp left turn into the then gateway of the Cricket Salts. The Salts were covered by what seemed a thousand or more soldiers of the Manchester Regiment. Field Marshall Montgomery had arrived to review these men. I left my cycle and joined a few other civilians there already, and so's not to miss this, we stood in the background, but close enough to hear. By now Monty was standing up in a jeep, waving his arms and calling for the men to gather round, "No formalities!" He introduced himself and said in a speech words to the effect that each man from the top of his command to the lowest and youngest private were to know their role, each was to be a participant when the time came for the coming battle.

I remember the "three cheers for Monty". I quickly left for home and a late dinner!

Some time later, it must have been late May, I noticed that the Manchester's vehicles had suddenly been replaced by new ones. Soon after our town seemed deserted, that is by the military.

The Royal Navy was still with us and also the anti aircraft units.

COMMANDOES : SPRING 1944

During this period there were times when Combined Operations Commandoes were frequently in the town, although to my knowledge, not garrisoned here.

THE ROYAL NAVY IN RYE

1942: I am unable to separate the events that took place when the Admiralty decided to improve Rye Harbour and make it fit to contribute to the course of the war.

In my lowly job as a chain boy, I was aware that a great deal of work was then in hand. In the initial period, contractors were engaged to reconstruct the harbour's western groyne, which had become very weak and in poor condition. Shingle that should have been collecting at the groyne was spilling into the harbour mouth. Other contractors were using two suction dredgers, "The Ballot'. and "Barge 50", to dredge the channel from the village to the sea.

1943: A great deal of civil engineering work was also in hand constructing: two concrete slipways, one at Strand Quay and one at Rye Harbour Village; a long timber jetty on the eastern side of the river, with facilities to refuel ships and landing craft the fuel being supplied from a branch of the "Pluto" pipe line that crossed the Marsh to Dungeness; and there were large gasometer like fuel storage tanks on the river frontage at Rye Harbour Village.

At the Fishmarket, a large star shaped concrete construction was built, whereby landing craft could be hauled up a slipway on large steel cradles running on rails, to a turn-table, where the craft could then be run back onto one of the many arms. This was to facilitate repairs to damaged craft by the Rother Iron Works/Steelyard. I only ever saw one landing craft hauled up this slip - I think, just for a test run.

Mr Johns was now living with us. He was employed by the Admiralty as a Clerk of Works, so I would think he was quite a busy man.

The naval personnel arrived and took over the Senior School which had been unoccupied since evacuation. It was named H.M.S.Haig. A row of about twelve Nissan huts was erected to take more naval ratings and they stood parallel to the footpath to the west of the school.

From my bedroom window I witnessed life in the Royal Navy. The flag raising ceremony took place every morning - a flag party would march out to the flag staff, consisting of an officer, a boatswain, a rating carrying the folded flag ready to raise it. Two other ratings gave the general salute with rifles. This was repeated in reverse at sunset.

A ship's bell, hung on a white metal frame by the flag standard, was rung through the day to change the watches. There was constant shrilling of boatswain's whistles as they walked the open corridors. (The bell is still at Freda Gardham School).

The Camber Tram at this time had a new lease of life, having been laid up for the duration of the war in 1939. It was now running again, manned by sailors, carrying men and materials to Rye Harbour daily. On fine summer evenings, it was a common sight to watch two or three petty officers as they paced up and down the flat roof of our woodwork classroom, as though they were on the deck of a ship, chatting for quite lengthy periods.

1944: Tank landing craft were now becoming quite a common sight in the river.

A number of W.R.N.S (Wrens) were then using 31 New Road for sleeping quarters, as the old lady who lived there had left at the height of the Battle of Britain. One afternoon, some Wrens were cycling down our road to this house. They found themselves within a convoy of American army lorries and it was pretty obvious that some horse play was going on, for, when one lorry was overtaking them, it collided with two British army lorries coming in the opposite direction. It overturned, but in doing so, it fell onto one British lorry and the other spun into our front garden fence.

One morning at work, I, with a colleague, attended a small meeting with the Harbour Master, Mr J.Doust at Strand Quay. Here we met a Royal Navy Officer, and the sight of a large tank landing craft with its bow on top of the Quay's concrete coping and its stern sitting on the river bottom at about a 60º angle, with the tide out. The problem was that when the tide returned, it would fill the stern before floating the craft. It was decided to call in the R.E.M.E. (Royal Electrical and Mechanical Engineers), who maintained a depot and workshop in the Rye Station Approach for the repair of military vehicles, in the requisitioned Maidstone and District Bus Garage.

A large recovery vehicle was brought to the far side of the Quay and, as the tide returned, a hawser attached to the craft's bow, was then gently pulled. As the stern gained buoyancy, it fell with a mighty splash. The scored concrete coping remains to this day, about 15m from the south east end of the quay, on the town side.

AIRCRAFT INVASION STRIPES : JUNE 4TH 1944

On the 4th of June I noticed suddenly that our aircraft were now showing very conspicuous black and white stripes. What could this mean?

D DAY : JUNE 6TH 1944

In my records of the numbers and type of aircraft seen on this day - D Day - they show no change in the pattern - not even a Dakota transport passed over.

The black and white stripes were painted on all Allied aircraft to give easy recognition to our forces, both on the ground and in the air.

THE CRASH OF A JUNKERS 88

I had left the house in New Road to walk the dog at about 10pm. On reaching Monkbretton Bridge, my interest was suddenly aroused by the searchlights in the direction of Winchelsea. The beams formed a great apex of light and, not as was generally the case, when the searchlights would just probe the night sky in twos and threes. I watched the point of the beams as they were moving in unison in my direction, until I could see an aircraft "trapped" in the light. Overhead now, I could see the shape of a Junkers 88 twin engined bomber. But within an instant, a mighty burst of machine gun and cannon fire crackled in the night sky. An unseen British night fighter had arrived to make its kill. The aircraft seemed to roll violently, the searchlights stayed with it, but as it continued eastwards, it was falling in a long descending flight. The light beams were now becoming flatter, but keeping it within their sights. Eventually the lights were gone and I assumed that it had crashed towards Brookland.

It was convenient to be working in a job like mine, visiting the land drainage excavators working on the Marsh.

On the following morning, we made enquiries in Brookland, and were directed to Kings Street Lane. Approaching the railway level crossing there, we saw a number of people were gathered. Stopping, we got out of the car to look through the open gate. Between the high thorn hedges there was a very large crater, almost undermining the rail crossing keeper's cottage. Amid the debris of the Junkers 88, were the mutilated bodies of the crew. I do not know why, but at the time, I just was not expecting to see this - the reality of war!

THE FLYING BOMBS :Doodlebugs: V.I's: The "KIWI'S"

D Day was now behind us and all was much quieter. The troops had all but left the town, except for the anti aircraft gun and searchlight crews, who could be seen from time to time. The military convoys were no longer a feature of our roads, but there was still a very strong presence of the Royal Navy at H.M.S.Haig.

JUNE 13TH 1944. I remember very well being awakened at dawn by the sound of a very noisy aircraft. I nipped to look out of the front bedroom window and for a few moments I watched a small plane travelling northwards in the direction of Iden. Flames were coming from its tail. As it passed out of view, the sound of it gradually faded, and I recall thinking well it hasn't crashed yet!"

JUNE 16TH 1944. On Sunday night, all of us in the house were awakened by a number of noisy aircraft passing over. They were not the sound of normal aircraft as they had a steady, deep and loud pulsating rhythm. It was the same noise that I had heard three days before. We all left our beds and thought it best to get in the Morrison table shelter, my older sister included. She was home on a long weekend leave from the W.A.A.F., and from her we learned that, in her work, information had been circulated that our country was to be attacked by a German secret weapon. Was this it?

The day started quietly enough, we had breakfast and then again that sound; another one was coming. Quickly I went to the back door and between the grey scudding clouds of a breezy morning, I caught just a glimpse of a small aircraft travelling very fast.

At work that morning it was all we could talk about and during that day, I spotted six of them. The fact of attacks by these weapons was broadcast on the radio, but no details were given.

The "Flying Bombs" had arrived, nicknamed "Doodle Bug" - an expression first coined by New Zealand fighter pilots.

The air activity over Rye now took on a completely different role - squadrons of the new Hawker Tempest fighter plane had flown into

Newchurch, Romney Marsh Airfield, stationed there to combat the flying bomb. My first sightings of this plane was on 18th April, and in that month I counted 11. In May the total was 33, then up to June 15th, there were 6 and on June 16th alone, I saw 40 of them.

The Tempests had arrived, and also an assortment of aircraft which were to fight the flying bomb. Always defending in pairs, Spitfires and Mustangs included, they patrolled the coastline, probably not flying more than 4 miles in any one direction, backwards and forwards, during the hours of daylight, every day, waiting to pounce upon an incoming flying bomb.

Only when an aircraft spotted a bomb approaching to cross its path, was it able to consider a chase, their speed being almost identical. If a bomb was spotted, and was likely to cross behind the patrol, they did not pursue, for it required the fighter to turn around, thereby losing time.

From our point of view in Rye, it was apparent that if the chasing aircraft was not successful in shooting down the bomb, it would give up the chase roughly over Iden/Peasmarsh. Then the planes quickly returned to the coast to resume their patrol. To see aircraft chasing a bomb, for me, was a very exciting experience. When in range, a burst of machine gun and cannon fire would blow up the bomb in the air, causing a huge ball of fire smoke and falling black debris.

One particular evening I watched a Tempest doing this, but the pilot was unable to avoid the exploding bomb. From where I stood in New Road, the bomb was somewhere over the Town Salts / Cricket Salts. The Tempest banked to the right having gone through the explosion - it passed in front of Point Hill, smoking as it went to crash at Boonshill Farm, on the Military Road. The pilot's plexiglass canopy fell in Fishmarket Road and wreckage of this plane was recovered in the 1970's and taken to the Aviation Museum at Brenzett. The New Zealand pilot was killed.

So numerous were these chases that I will only recall a few of them here. Aircraft chasing bombs could be very scary, especially if it was coming in your direction, for when hit, the aerobatics would be very unpredictable. I watched one lose a wing going towards Iden from East Guldeford. It continued horizontal flight, but spun end on, to crash on a house in Grove Lane, killing some of its occupants. On two occasions I saw a bomb turn on its tail and go vertically out of sight, which left me wondering where it had come down. One lunchtime I watched a disabled bomb falling. It exploded on a house at the Mount, Military Road. I remember the Navy driving out of the school gate to go to the scene of the explosion and assist. Here again was a fatality and a house destroyed.

Whilst working at Rye Harbour, near the river mouth, I watched a disabled bomb coming from Camber. It passed over to make a perfect landing in the Nook Beach, now the Bird Reserve, but on touching down, it set off a long string of buried landmines, which had been lying there since 1940. What a spectacular sight that was!

I will give just one more experience. Cycling with three other teenage friends on a Saturday afternoon to see the aircraft at Newchurch Airfield, we rounded the Kent Ditch Corner beyond East Guldeford. Looking towards the coast, we spotted a number of flying bombs coming in from the sea. This was a frequent ploy by the Germans to saturate the fighter defences. We stood in the road watching - one bomb was coming towards us and a Mustang fighter was chasing it, giving it a long burst of machine gun fire and then it banked away. It left the bomb, now descending, coming towards us. Its ram jet engine had now stopped. We ran for cover in the road side ditch. As we crouched there it passed low over our heads to crash and explode a few hundred yards away in the field. What a fright? We quickly ran across to the smoking shallow crater, lying to one side was the still glowing red hot steel ram jet engine All around us were dead birds killed by the blast. We never went to look at the airfield but turned and cycled home.

People locally began to realise that the incoming bombs tended to be flying along a fixed line. In fact, it could be said there were five separate tracks across the Rye area. These bombs were being launched from ramps in northern France, their course being consistent with the ramps' fixed direction. They would cross over Rye at an altitude of roughly 2000 feet, really not very high, and occasionally too low.

On 4th July 1944, in the late evening at about 11pm, the weather was, as I remember, quite appalling, blowing and raining hard. We were sitting in our Morrison Shelter listening to bombs passing over. Then there was another throbbing, away in the distance, it suddenly exploded, then silence. This to us was different, we had never heard a bomb do that before. The majority of the town's people were to find out the following morning that this bomb had literally flown directly into either Cadborough Farm House, or the ground in front of it with one fatality, Major Hacking. [*in fact a soldier manning a gun emplacement by the house, was also killed, Ed.*]

The low altitude of the bomb's flight may have been due to weather conditions or a failure of its flight mechanism. There were, to my knowledge, two other examples where this occurred, one exploding into the high bank between Boonshill and Iden Lock and the other into the high headland of the Isle of Oxney, near Knocke Bridge between Iden Lock and Appledore.

To recap "Bombing of Northern France, Summer 1943", the flying bomb launching ramps were often the unknown targets of the medium bombers of the American 9th Army Airforce, passing over Rye. The bombs weighed two tons, had a wing span of 4.8m, length 7.7m and had a speed of 350 mph.

A change was taking place, the fighter aircraft were still chasing bombs, but it was realised that a large percentage of flying bombs were escaping inland through the defences and adding to the fighter aircraft's problems. The small local anti aircraft gums of Rye were joining in the action against the bombs even when a bomb was being chased. It appeared that co-ordination was lacking between the air and military forces,

Between July 13th and 16th, extraordinary activities were taking place on the roads into, and through Rye. Heavy military and private contractors' vehicles were seen towing heavy anti aircraft guns and trailers of equipment to back them up.

Eight of these guns were set up in the first field to the right hand side of New Road, beyond the houses there, and just beyond the Borough boundary. It had a conspicuously large radar van and its accompanying aerials, and also a large tented area for the gun crews.

This was repeated in the second field on the right in Rye Harbour Road, just beyond Brede Sluice. Here the 40mm Bofors gun of Rye's permanent defence was on the left.

Another eight were sited at Moneypenny Farm East Guldeford, and another group at Blue House, a site some 1.5 miles beyond the Woolpack Inn. Brookland, on the road to Lydd. Yet another set was in what was recently Maddison's Holiday Camp, Camber. Here the eight guns were crewed by A.T.S. girls. They were also under canvas (tents), but they did have the use of the camp's community hall and other remaining amenities.

How did I know all this? In the course of my work, I often found myself in or around them. In an area 4 miles square there were 40 of these particular guns, which will give some idea of their concentration. But I'm not finished listing the new defences - at Rye Harbour, by the Martello Tower, was a Z battery of racked rocket launchers and from Pett Level to Jury's Gap on the coast were countless 40 mm Bofors and the RAF. Regiment's small armoured vehicles carrying pairs of heavy machine guns.

This concentration of armament, history now tells us, stretched from Hastings to Folkestone - in all some 1500 anti aircraft guns of all types, all within a three mile belt of land, parallel to the sea. Its official name was "Operation Diver", due to the diving attitude of the bomb once its engine had stopped on reaching its target. (That was London).

The patrolling aircraft were now withdrawn and set to patrol inland of Rye. The guns had to take on the sole defence against the bombs, and the aircraft were to pick up those that escaped the gun barrage.
I am able to give my reader some idea of the events that we, in Rye, were witnessing, as I would spend many an hour sitting on the flat shed roof in our garden - on the fine summer evenings and weekends

of July and August 1944, waiting and watching for the guns to go into action - at times looking towards the gunsite beyond the end of the houses in our road, some 300m away.

Suddenly and silently the gun barrels would elevate just a little, and instantly commence firing. The roar of the guns was really deafening, not only these guns, but every gun in the vicinity.

Away on the horizon there was nothing to mar my view. I would see the little black puffs of exploding shells and, by now, the noise engulfed the mind. The interest now was to watch the distant action, as the 9.4cm calibre guns would each be pumping out shells at the rate of 25 a minute.

Multiply this by eight, and then by the rest of the heavy guns, and add the various assortment of smaller guns, (the 40 mm Bofors output was 120 shells a minute), and finally,if this wasn't enough, add the searing noise of the Z battery rocket launchers by the Martello Tower at Rye Harbour. Rockets could be fired at the rate of 9 in 3/4 of a second, this may give you some idea of the noise the barrage created.

The puffs, now tightly packed together, would form a black cloud rapidly coming closer, growing at the speed of the unseen bomb, probably at 350 miles per hour. The cloud was like a great monster - an elongated column of black smoke, beginning to thin, turning grey and drifting out on the horizon. Its length could now be 3 miles long.

I was looking all the time to see the speeding bomb, and then seeing it plainly coming into view, just keeping ahead of the exploding shell bursts. The sound of the bomb's ram jet engine was completely drowned by the barrage, and then suddenly there was a large ball of fire. More black smoke and the pieces of debris from the disintegrating flying bomb burst out of the fire ball. Instantly the guns would cease and then there was incredible silence. But it was common enough to find 2 or 3 more bombs speeding landward, ahead of their exploding smoke trails, yet to be annihilated.

All gun fire would generally cease once a bomb was over the built up areas of the town, but I'm not sure that that was the reason, or whether it was because the landward limit of the gun belt had been reached. There were times that when a bomb was approaching overhead, it was a case of "run for cover" - standing in doorways as the sound of shrapnel was plainly heard tinkling on the roofs, pavements, and roads - probably because the gun crews were becoming a little exuberant so as not to let the bomb escape. I do not ever recall anyone being injured by falling debris, but it was very possible.

Imagine this repeated in the darkness of the blackout, standing, as I have done many times, in the bedroom window, watching the greatest firework display ever - tracer shells arching up from all directions on the ground, to the little flaming points of light speeding through the sky towards Rye - then almost always a ball of fire - and then it was all over.

As the days passed into August, the flying bombs were becoming more numerous, but the guns were also becoming more accurate. Only a small percentage was getting through the defence line.

At work on the Marsh, it could be very scary at times as there was nowhere to take shelter other than under the odd farm crossing bridge, or lying within the banks of a ditch, not that this gave much shelter. It was now becoming very common to find, anywhere on the Marsh, the little black plastic shell nose cones. History now tells us that the reason for accuracy by gun crews was that the shells were now fitted with a new proximity fuse in the nose cap.

It was said by locals generally, "If only the Londoners could see the success the gun crews were having!" The news bulletins on the radio made very little reference to flying bomb activity, so as not to let the enemy know what effect they were having.

A very unfortunate incident occurred on the Blue House, Brookland gun site. A bomb, disabled by gun fire (a rare event as they were usually destroyed), actually crashed and exploded amid the tented area of the gun crews, killing and wounding a number of soldiers and A.T.S. girls.

To cater for the hundreds of men and women of the Royal Artillery, two very large marquees were erected on the Cricket Salts, parallel to New Road - one a N.A.A.F.I. (Navy, Army, Air Force, Institute) canteen and the other a type of concert hall, run by an organisation known as E.N.S.A. (Entertainments National Service Association).

We teenagers would find our way in by crawling under the canvas sides when shows were in progress. These facilities were to give some light relief to the weary gun crews who were manning the guns 24 hours a day.

By late August, the British forces were advancing across northern France, over-running the flying bomb sites. It is very possible that even some of the army divisions that had been stationed in Rye, were now doing this.

SEPTEMBER/OCTOBER/NOVEMBER 1944

Our danger was now rapidly passing - the last flying bomb that I recorded was on August 30th. No more were seen and the guns remained for a few weeks and then were cleared. During this period, the site crew at Rye Harbour Road stacked all their empty brass cartridge cases on the roadside to await collection. It is no exaggeration to say they were in stacks, mostly in boxes, 2m or more high and roughly 100m long in two blocks. I passed them a number of times and thought I must have one for a souvenir, so during one dark evening, I cycled there, armed with a sack, and took one. I was rather taken aback by the weight and it was 100 mm in diameter and 1m high, when standing on end. It remained in our shed for a number of years and then I took it to the Camber side of Rye Harbour and hung it up there, to be used as a gong to call the ferryman.

CALL UP : SEPTEMBER/ OCTOBER NOVEMBER 1944

These months were uneventful, as far as war was concerned in Rye, but not for me. I received my call-up papers to report to Preston Barracks, Brighton, for a military service medical. I wanted to Join the RAF, but at this time, due to the late stage of the war, recruiting was only for the army. There was also a chance I might be drawn in a National Lottery for service in the coal mines, whose winners were known as Bevin Boys.

But, luck was with me, for on the day my final call up came, it read "Report to Cardington, Bedfordshire." A very few days after my 18th birthday - November 30th - I was in the Royal Air Force. Therefore I did not witness the end of hostilities and the celebrations, if any, in Rye on V.E.Day.

UNITED SERVICE OF THANKSGIVING

United service of Thanksgiving was held on the Cricket Salts, Rye at 3p.m. on the Day after V-Day.

A Boat showing the Rye and Hastings registration
at Rye Harbour today

Wartime Memories of David Cade

I was four years old when war was declared and had just started at the Rye Collegiate School Kindergarten. I can remember my parents listening to the radio, presumably to the announcement of hostilities, in a very sombre mood. Shortly after there were tears from my mother and some excitement from my father; I have no recollection of understanding what was afoot, but I asked my sister (who was nearly thirteen) why my mother was crying. We soon found out when my father appeared in army uniform and there were anguished goodbyes. I now know he went off to join the British Expeditionary Force. After arriving in France, the authorities caught up with his (exemplary) record, but which showed his medical discharge from the regular army after two doses of severe gassing in the First World War, and he was sent home.

Back in Rye, he became Quartermaster and second in command of the Rye Home Guard, which was a large contingent led by a Captain Plews. All the Rye men still here were in it and to look at a photograph of them marching down Landgate is like looking at a pictorial 'who's who' of the town at that time.

As we know, nothing much happened until nearly a year later, in 1940, and by then I was fully aware of events, and although memories are nearly complete, several different happenings stand out. The continual air raids which were initially terrifying but later became ordinary - a part of everyday life; the sound of aircraft engines at which we all became experts in recognising friend or foe; the sight of the German pilots and crew looking down at you. This sounds exaggerated but in fact these bombers often returned across the Channel at a very low level, I suppose about 100 ft., and you really could clearly see them. There were vast number of soldiers around and batteries of anti-aircraft guns everywhere, with batteries of searchlights in attendance. I recall the excitement of seeing an aircraft caught in the cross beams of searchlights and the tracer shells from the guns; the sound of the ubiquitous Bren gun carrier rumbling round the roads, and the sight of trains with tanks and armoured cars aboard slowly puffing across the Marsh. Snaring rabbits on the old Camber Castle Golf Course with my father to supplement the meat supply, seeing the wonderful Shire horse that pulled the railway delivery cart around the town; the horses working in the fields, not many tractors then; and the haystacks so expertly built, are all clear in my mind. Then there was the barbed wire and the tank traps. Barbed wire was everywhere. It was forbidden to go on the beach, and if you got near at all, you could see there were row upon row of barbed wire fences. Even the Camber Tram was used by the military and frequently sported a Lewis gun on an armoured truck. These are general memories but some are more specific.

There was the day when I was at home from school as usual for lunch and realised that I was going to be late back. My mother insisted I leave my pudding and get off. Running most of the way back, I passed P.C.Fowler outside Roses (now Jempson's) at the bottom of Market Road. We spoke as I passed and, as I reached the bottom of Conduit Hill, there was an almighty explosion. I should mention that there was an air-raid in progress and the policeman and I were the only people on the streets. I was carried by the blast some sixty feet up the hill, fell and rolled in the dust and scampered, somewhat bruised, into school through the back gate. This was the bomb on the cinema and the policeman, having seen me only a minute before, looked for me in the rubble and dust and made an assumption that I must be under it. He went up to my father and told him to expect the worst. Father rushed home to break the news there and you can imagine my surprise to find them comforting each other when I walked in couple of hours later. My sister, of course, was no longer at home, having been evacuated with the Grammar School to Bedford for the duration.

One day early in the war my father was out on patrol with the Home Guard. It must have been early, because it was before they were issued with rifles; shot guns provided with horrific cartridges with a single ball in them, and pitchforks were more usual, or any other lethal weapons which came to hand. I remember it was a fine day and I had been feeding the chicken, (everyone had chicken, as it was the only way to get eggs; dried eggs were the norm), when my father and two HG's escorted a man in full flying gear into our kitchen. It turned out that he was German fighter pilot who had been shot down just up the Tillingham Valley and was captured by our three heroes as his parachute touched down. I remember frantic phone calls to headquarters to discover what to do with him, but above all this, I remember my mother's concern for his health and would he like a cup of tea? There they sat in the kitchen with tea and cake, with me standing in a corner waiting for the Military Police to take the prisoner away!

Talking of shooting down reminds me of the battery of Bofors guns in what were known as the 'fattin fields' (now the Tilling Green Estate), in front of our house in the Old Brickyard. The gunners often got very enthusiastic, and depressed the guns so low, trying to hit the low flying planes heading home, that on two occasions they shot our chimney down, resulting in embarrassed CO's visits to apologise, and form filling to get them rebuilt.

The worst thing that happened at home was the day the bombs fell on our house. The air raid siren had sounded, so we all went outside to see what was about. One has to realise that the air raid sirens were sounded both ways, when the planes were incoming on their way to a raid probably on London, and on their way back, often being chased by our fighters, and keen to unload any bombs still on board before crossing the Channel. The speed of these happenings by today's standards was quite slow, so there was often time to take in the situation before heading for an air raid shelter.

On this occasion the planes were fairly high and we could see them releasing bombs and watch them fall. They were definitely coming our way and my mother grabbed me and we rushed for the cupboard under the stairs, which for some unknown reason, was the haven universally believed by all to be the safest. This was before we were issued with a Morrison shelter, which was a steel indoor device.

Everything then happened at once; my father literally flew inwards down the hall and was knocked out on the cloakroom door; I received an almighty thump on my right shoulder and was thrown down on top of my mother, who was smothered by the contents of a laundry basket in the cupboard we were sharing. It transpired that I had received a glancing blow from the bomb as it crashed right though the centre of the house and down through the oversite into the marshy land below. Fortunately it didn't explode! I remember staring at the huge hole in the floor, before helping my father, and putting distance between the house and us. Our neighbours had watched the fall of the bombs all the way and were the first to come and, of course, offer us a cup of tea. They dug for three days but could not catch up with the bomb; then they were called away to do something more urgent, so poured thirty tons of concrete in the hole and left.

We had a period when the German fighters would rush in low and strafe anything that moved. The reason was that the whole area was like a huge army camp. This, by the way, was very beneficial to young lads good at scrumping; the bored troops on endless route marches were more than willing to give a penny for an apple or a pear! Anyway, there was my father and I walking through the fields, having been mushrooming, when a German fighter comes towards us fifty feet above the ground and we saw the terrible puffs from the machine guns and the ground leaping up in front of us. My father grabbed me and leaped into the adjacent ditch. We were unharmed, though very wet, but it was a close run thing.

I seem to have a lot of near misses. About 1944, I was stood on Longley's Corner, the junction of Cinque Port Street and Ferry Road, waiting for my father to get a new pair of shoes from Swan's. A Canadian Artillery convoy with guns on carriages was going round the corner on its way from exercises back to their camp at the top of Udimore Road. One took the bend too sharply and came onto the pavement and knocked me down. It broke both my legs and, when they got me home, they took my balaclava off to find it was soaking with blood, as my head was badly cut and no one had noticed. I had broken the shop window with my head. Dr Mannington came to sort me out.

Later, when the V I flying bombs appeared, I was playing in the same field as the 'ditch' incident, and watching the tracer from the guns attempting to hit one of these bombs not far overhead. They were never very high, and this one must have been hit, for the engine cut out, and it turned and headed straight towards us. We both ran and attempted to hide behind a large ash tree. The bomb fell and exploded just fifty feet the other side of the tree and we were unharmed. Being curious and, before going home, we went round to gather a few fragments as trophies, which I still have. The tree and crater are also still there. The strange sound of the jet engines in the flying bombs, which did not sound as we now know jet engines to sound, was one of the most memorable things in the war. Not a pleasant one, but something that evokes fear. When the engine stopped, where was the explosion to be? The worst of these in Rye was one that never gained height and went straight into Cadborough Farm at the top of Udimore Road and sadly killed Major Hacking.

There are many more thoughts and memories. Going to Dover one day and experiencing shells falling from guns across the Channel, and an outing organised by the Curate of Rye Harbour to a theatre in London, when, no sooner had we left the front door, than a bomb fell and demolished the stage. All the iron railings being cut down and reused for the war effort; this was very noticeable in Rye, which had railings in abundance, presumably because of the Rother Iron Works.

I remember watching the building of Admiralty MFV's at G&T Smith's shipyard round in Rock Channel, and the last of the sailing trawlers, the 'Three Brothers' laid up in the Strand Quay. Incidentally this boat was wrecked in Ireland only five years ago. One of the only boats that fished during the war was the 'Arthur', also in Strand Quay, because the Fishmarket and Admiralty Quay were used by the Admiralty for coastal forces. I recall attending Sunday School, which was held in the lower hall at the United Reformed Church, now the kitchen, chapel and hall of the Community Centre. The cattle being loaded and unloaded from cattle trucks at the market and the market itself with rabbits, goats, pigs, chicken, cattle and sheep. There was the smell of the railway-shunting yard, a strange sickly sweet smell; gas masks and having to carry them round at all times, and the black-out with wardens who would be knocking on the door if a glimmer of light showed. All the shop fronts sandbagged to prevent damage from blast and special covers with slits in for the car and lorry headlights. There are so many memories and I shall end on just two more.

Rye Collegiate School was run by the Misses Moon and, for the duration of the war, took boys beyond the normal Kindergarten age while all ages of girls were catered for. Now the air raid shelter was down the garden at the rear and what fun we horrible small boys had with a trip wire and the girls on the way there. There was a teacher whose real name I do not know, but we knew her as 'Fanny Gasbags'. She claimed to know the sound of all aeroplanes and whether they were friend or foe. This was presumably useful as we did not always go to the bomb shelter and sometimes she was not in time. She allocated us places to shelter in the classroom and mine was under the grand piano with three others. I have often wondered how we would have survived if the sheer weight of the piano had fallen on us, but then these were things we never considered and perhaps that's just as well.

A B17 Flying Fortress

The Memories of Alan Catt

I was eight when War broke out and lived at New Bentley, the middle of the three houses as you enter the Camber Road at East Guldeford. My grandfather was farming at Moneypenny Farm.

My father farmed and I, as a child, was aware of the pressure of work on him. Before the War, we were 100% Sheep and, when war broke out, half our flocks were compulsorily purchased. We were compelled to plough half the farm. Any farmer who didn't cooperate had his farm taken over and the East Sussex War Agricultural Committee farmed it. Land Girls were brought in to help on these farms as well as helping on other ones.

We had no machinery for arable work and the Ministry of Agriculture tried to provide a pool of machinery for farmers to hire. The depot was the Wool Store (previously my great-uncle had milked cows in that building). It is now the part of Skinner's Garage where the 'cars for sale' are parked.

In the early days of the war we had ready a small attaché sized suitcase packed with a change of underclothes - for mother and I to be evacuated should there be an invasion. Father would be left behind. It was planned we would get via Brooke's Gate to Iden where we would get transport North. My mother had a slab of chocolate in the case - which we ate later in the war to celebrate the recapture of Torbruk- a very real treat! On the Sunday War was declared, the village was digging in. The East Guldeford Parish Meeting Minute Book (from 1896) described: *Air Raids were planned; Gas masks are to be sent to Moneypenny to be fitted.* I remember that if they 'snorted like a pig' when you exhaled they were all right. A square of tissue paper was the test on the snout when you inhaled - if it fell off, the straps were not tight enough.

A Communal dug-out was dug between St John's Cottages and the corner of the A 259, on the old sea wall, by the men of the village. We used it until Anderson and Morrison shelters arrived.

Father built our own air raid shelter in the garden where we slept in our clothes during the nights of the London raids. Later I slept under the stairs at New Bentley for most of the war. But when things got quieter and we slept in our own beds indoors, we were very careful to put our clothes near the bed and laid in the right order so that we could easily dress in the dark. This was done every night of the war because you never knew what might happen and also you couldn't put a light on because of the blackout restrictions: or there might also be a power cut.

When the troops came back from Dunkirk they were pretty shattered and some were billeted in The Mount - which was empty.

We had a Howitzer in our farm buildings. It pointed to the sea - but they only fired practice shots at the beginning of the war.

My father was in charge of the local Home Guard - a real Captain Mainwaring. He used to say he had every character in that programme was in his platoon. The Home Guard observation post was at Blackhouse Farm. His area was East Guldeford and Rye to the east of Monkbretton Bridge - i.e. Kings Avenue and New Road. This was because the bridge would have been blown in the event of invasion and so that part of Rye would have been with East Guldeford. All the bridges were prepared for blowing - and a very jumpy army officer actually blew up some of the bridges round here - at Brooks Gate, Boons Hill and Knock, and they had to be replaced by bailey bridges. Most were rebuilt immediately after the war, but, in fact, the one at Brook's Gate (by the Baker's) was only replaced recently.

My father's parents lived at Iden Lock and father had to go to and fro - it really inconvenienced him as he had to go around Rye.
Sometimes I used to watch the Home Guard training - before they got their uniforms. Father built a 2.2 rifle range at Salts Farm. The ordinary service rifle was a 303 - and they used 303 rifles with Morrison tubes, which took 2.2 only, just for practice. They later moved to a full sized range at Camber Castle.

They also used to throw dummy hand grenades, and exercise at night. Ammunition and guns were sometimes delivered at night too. The Browning machine guns came caked in solid grease. We had a bucket of paraffin in the sitting room to clean them - my mother was having forty fits about the condition of her carpet! I can hear one old boy now saying, " If you would be so good as to read the instructions backwards, we'll try to put them together again!" The HQ at Rye, in the old Drill Hall, was run by ex 1914-18 old soldiers who were N.C.O.s and Officers, and who knew what they were doing. These old Soldiers used to tell wonderful stories of Army life. Father had been on the O.T.C. when he was away at school. He always liaised with the local Regiment and, after Dunkirk, one Officer told him, "Don't put men in the pill boxes" - there was one at North Point - "The Germans are using flame throwers."

A Searchlight arrived at East Guldeford, and, as they said during the war, "I have to put it here!" 'Here' was by the Old Vicarage. My father said, "That's a damn silly place - it will be wet in winter!" Eventually sense prevailed and they said, "Can you find us anywhere drier?" They then went to the bank in front of Moneypenny, which was slightly higher. There were several attempts to bomb this search-light without success.

The Radar Station was built at Brookland - it was started before the War. Apart from watching its construction, I remember seeing the Autogiro, which was used to set it up. It was rather like a micro light - and had revolving wings like a helicopter. It was used to get the direction finder accurately placed. I was very intrigued - remember it was the time of H.G. Wells 'Power Ray' stories - there were all sorts of rumours about it. The Civil Engineers were billeted with other radar specialists on us and others, whilst the construction work was going on, but they never talked about their work.

Originally there were four wood and four steel pylons towers, but they took down one of the steel ones. The next Station was at Pevensey to the west, at and Dover to the east.

There were two attempts to bomb the station in one day, one in the morning and one in the evening. There was terrible confusion and noise but they missed the towers. I remember being in the farmyard with my father feeding the animals during the evening raid.

It was all quite exciting for us kids - or terrifying - especially during the Battle of Britain. We watched vapour trails, parachutes and aircraft coming down amid the sheaves of wheat on hot sunny days. Trains with tanks, lorries and guns going by were common sights.
Sometimes my father would take me to see a bomb hole or crashed aircraft. A Spitfire landed in our largest field in 1940. I was coming home from School by bus that day. Father got on and paid extra to take me half way to what is now the Windsurfing School to where the old sea wall had a hedge on the top, on the right hand side. There was a Spitfire sitting in the field. The pilot was sitting by its side. He had been one of two patrolling having been scrambled from Manston very early in the morning to go to Dunkirk. He had his pyjamas on under his flying jacket. He'd run out of fuel and, subsequently after refuelling, we took out a bit of fence and he took off, doing a wonderful exhibition of aerobatics. The Police had taken him to Bennett's and bought him trousers and shirt for £2.10s, which they lent him. He subsequently wrote a cheque payable to Rye Police Station and they wrote back saying, "Have this one on us!" and tore up the cheque!

The two pilots had been trying to get back to Manston in fog. His colleague went to Tangmere, but he hadn't enough fuel and so landed. They were instructed to keep their landing gear up when landing - as the air frames were easy to repair - but landing gear damaged the plane much more. It was a Court-Marshal offence to land wheels down in an emergency - but our pilot had landed and taken off successfully with wheels down. He wrote about the incident in the official log "You have got your pilot and your plane!" I met the pilot in the 1980's and he said he'd only been to Rye twice - once in his plane and the second time then, to find the field where he landed 40 years ago!

After that incident, the Ministry of Defence came and dug trenches across the field ruining the complex land drainage system, which had been put in the 1860's. My father was horrified. Subsequently they filled in the trenches and put in poles with 'A' frames at each end and posts in between. Old cables from collieries were laid across the top. This meant we could cultivate beneath them. Sometimes the poles were of willow and they began to grow! Other large grass fields had just large poles put all over them. This was to prevent German aircraft/gliders from landing.

On another occasion when father was lambing early, on the horizon he saw a little aircraft, an Auster. When he cautiously approached, he found the pilot asleep. He said he'd got a bit lost and so landed to wait for daylight and could do with some breakfast. After that - he took off!

Father had a constant problem with the troops pinching things, chickens, eggs, and especially driving mirrors, which they used for shaving mirrors!

Some soldiers helped with the harvest but they were useless. I remember going with father to St Anthony (taken over by the troops) to get some allocated for farm work.

The Freda Gardham School was at one time a convalescent home for wounded Petty Officers and they helped too. These sailors were much better - they were prepared to listen and learn. They were really good company too. Even though we were harvesting manually, we did it the easiest possible way. For example, we would hand the sheaves over a certain way, so that it would be easier to build the stack or load. The sailors understood - whereas the soldiers really didn't want to know!

All through the War, Peter Hickman and I attended Playden School - we walked or cycled. During the early part of the war a lot of stuff fell from the sky and so there was the risk of being hit!! We had a close call when Messerschmitt 109's flew down the river to Star Lock and Scots Float. We were coming home and had just got to the Brooks Gate when they shot up the lock gates with cannon, then bombed Rye and disappeared. My father must have worked out that we would have just been about there. We laughed for years after - for we threw ourselves into the ditch and then had to pull ourselves out! Father rushed to us on his bike - we said he would have won the "Tour de France" for his speed! Ammunition had rained round us and tears of relief that we were alright were running down the sides of his face.

Food for everyone was short. We were lucky as we had plenty of milk - all farmers' had a house cow at that time. We also had plenty of eggs, poultry and rabbits. When we used to harvest the fields, the reaper used to go round in a spiral from the outside to the inside. A lot of rabbits would be driven to the centre. If there were not many people around, we would shoot them, but if there were a lot of people, would put the guns down and run after them. The rabbits would hide under the sheaves! A local elderly roadman always knew exactly the place to be - so he could get a rabbit for dinner!

In 1940 or 1941, I remember being woken up to see, from the bedroom window, the glow in the sky when the invasion fleet at Boulogne was set alight. The invasion never came - it was a suicidal scheme - there were the climatic conditions to consider, never mind being shot. However we didn't know that then!

Another night - from another window we watched the Medway towns being bombed. We could see the tracers - it looked like fireworks and we felt sorry for the people who had a terrible time. When London was bombed we could see the glow of the fires in the sky.

No lights were to be shown at night, there were no street lights and bonfires only could be lit during the day - but we did have lovely star lit nights, and we became accustomed to them.

I remember the troops from the Searchlight Unit in 1940/1 singing carols around the piano at Moneypenny House - as well as bawdy military songs, which they toned down, for the company. The 'Quartermaster's Stores' was one of them!

Mother's sister used to drive a Mobile Canteen to the outlying searchlight positions - taking cups of tea and sandwiches to the men. She also used to sell razor blades and toothpaste. I used to go with her - mainly to open the gates in the fields.

My father was very forward thinking and had one of the few motor mowers made by West engineers. Mr West had made about thirty before the war, by taking the top off a car so as to use the chassis and driving gear to power the mower. It was the only piece of machinery we had before the War, but we did have a couple of old horses. It was a useful run-around, and a hay sweep (a large wooden comb which pushed the rows of hay up to the stack), and during the winter for light cultivation.

In 1940 we got a Standard Fordson tractor - petrol-paraffin. I was very involved in the farm within my limitations; I drove the tractor at age ten, but not on the road, and ploughed at fourteen.

I recall father assembling an imported Massey Harris plough straight out of a packing case - no instructions. He had never seen one before and he was pretty proud having succeeded. The same happened for a reaper and binder - if we hadn't got one we could borrow one from the Depot in Rye. We put them in 'cotton wool' after harvest!

The first day we used the reaper - on a field close to Rye, we had some teething problems. A Canadian military padre in a car stopped on the road and told us that we were a bar missing - we had been unable to find where it fitted! The bar was put on and we went on successfully.

Tip and Run raiders were trying to attack the fighter airfields and shoot up the trains. I think for morale boosting, there were a series of armoured cars - about six - with twin Vickers machine guns mounted on them, parked in daylight from Kings Avenue through East Guldeford; behind The Mount and on the double bend between the Level Crossings and Holme's sheep pens. The soldiers got bored and I used to talk to them on my way home from school. These soldiers were billeted at The Mount where a wooden building was constructed on the front lawn. Most houses in East Guldeford were occupied by farmers or farm workers - no commuters or retired people.

The resident Regiments came and went. Everyone loved the Canadians and all were deeply distressed after the Dieppe Raid.

Much of the farm help moved about, as skilled men were scarce. Land Girls worked with us, as did River Board men in the evenings at harvest time. These men were too old for military service and probably drove an excavator all day before coming to us. We had no combines then - we were told we had to put the corn stacks a set distance apart. This was so that incendiary bombs wouldn't set them alight all at once.

Mother applied and got extra rations for shepherds and employees at lambing and harvest. She gave the workers tea when they stayed on in the evenings. She would come out with two great cans of tea and sandwiches - with nothing in them but butter! We had 'double summer time' then, which meant long evenings.

We had lost a lot of skilled men such as engineers who were drafted away, for example to Short's Aircraft Factory at Rochester.

Not everyone was in the Home Guard; some were Special Constables; others were Air Raid Wardens; a few did nothing and they were somewhat despised. The Home Guard had to have a lecture on 'Gas Attacks'. The Instructors were pretty snappy for they were used to dealing with professional soldiers - not countrymen! One man questioned as to how long his boots should boil to decontaminate them from mustard gas - replied, hesitantly, "Until they were done!"

There were alerts for spies - posters and propaganda. We always listened to the 1 o'clock and 9 o'clock News on the radio. After the latter, and much later in the war, when all the National Anthems had been played, the messages for the French and Dutch resistance (in code) were read out.

There was a great deal of tension at the early part of the war. Some schools were evacuated - I nearly went to Australia to relations. Villagers were called up, some came back and others didn't, and some were POW's.

Village life went on much as usual. The Old School Room was the equivalent of a village hall and there were Whist Drives for the Red Cross and the Spitfire Fund. The house adjoining was let to an agricultural worker. Farm life went on too! There was always something happening here - military exercises of some sort. On one occasion before the Normandy Landings, the R.E.M.E. practiced recovering lorries - previously pushed into ditches - as an exercise. I learned a lot from just watching them.

Well before the Normandy Landings I saw a tank on a low-loader parked on the Camber Road corner - under a tarpaulin. Father and I were poking under it - "What is this?" An armed Lance Corporal moved us on smartly. It was quite a long time after that we discovered it was a prototype flail tank - with a bar in the front with chains to thrash the ground to explode mines. It was demonstrated before Churchill on Camber Sands, I believe. There were so many little mysteries in the war.

There was an incredible shortage of tyres, tubes and spare parts, which caused much anxiety. We cannibalised machinery for parts. West Engineers (Bill West and Jack Goodwin) - just beside the Wind Surfing School - were brilliant for repairs. The boost in agricultural machinery had not started then - and so we made some machinery ourselves, and wagons from car chassis etc. Drake and Fletcher at Ashford were good for spares.

The night raids on London were a terrifying time for me. The dreadful droning engines - and some had three of them - had a reverberating effect. We knew that if they got shot at, they would drop their load of bombs here on the way home. We could see London burning. One got to learn the points of the compass and we tried to judge how far away the raids were.

Much later in the war there were the daylight raids with the Super Fortresses on Germany. They were a disaster because they got shot up - great holes in their wings and engines not working etc. Some managed to get to the Marsh airfields - when they were out of fuel. They unloaded their wounded and set off again for their bases in East Anglia, some with only two engines and others with bits missing. I recall two Thunderbolts colliding on the Marsh.

We kids became very quick at aircraft recognition - there were posters everywhere with silhouettes and we all made models from scraps of wood. We could 'see' all round - not like farms with trees, hedges and hills so we had a good view of them.

The 'doodlebugs' were another thing. The first night they came over, father said stay inside, for it was a noise we had never heard before - and a sheet of flame. A neighbour, Harry Neeves, said "There's another alight - he'll come down in a minute". A few did come down here. One came down at the back of East Guldeford Church. I believe Mr Dunk was killed. Father was one of the official slaughter men - to kill wounded animals. He took mother's carving knife but many sheep were dead already.

When the 'doodlebugs' - the V I's started, a battery 3.7 Ack Ack guns arrived in New Road - in the field on the right as you leave Rye. We had not finished harvesting and they wouldn't wait. The map reference said "here" and that was that.

Father was a bit overcome by the numbers of people men and women that came with the guns. He said "they were the roughest batch of women I'd ever seen in my life!" These were the A.T.S. girls who manned the radar for the guns - but they did an excellent job.

There were also Bofors guns opposite the Harbour Master's Office at Saunders buildings. The big 3.7 guns shot out to sea; the Bofors were smaller and shot shells a lot more quickly - up to the vertical. The aircraft then picked it up from there. Once they fixed on the V I, they would go alongside it and tip the wing up.

When the 3.7 shot, the noise was phenomenal. I would be driving a tractor, (we had two by then!), with no cab or silencer, showered with shrapnel, which came down vertically. My father then got me a tin hat!! This was 1944.

These 3.7 guns were not very effective until they got the Magnetic/Proximity Shell. These didn't actually have to hit the object - but they made it go off when within so many feet. Then 99% were shot down. These 'doodlebugs' were much more frightening than the raids from aircraft because you never knew where they would come down. Once past, of course, YOU were alright!

I remember seeing Dakotas towing gliders for D Day Landings and for Arnhem. Planes with black and white stripes on their under wings. We were in a Restricted Area - and taking sheep out to winter keep was our only holiday/break. They were sent to the Lewes area by lorry and Jennings of the Beach Works ran two lorries which we used. I remember going through The Cross-in-Hand area and seeing the woods solid with troops and machinery and not knowing why. It was just before the Normandy Landing and they were being held back there to confuse the enemy into thinking that a second invasion would take place from this area.

Farm life was never the same again: pre-war we were nearly all sheep - but the introduction of arable farming and mechanisation has caused reduction of manpower ever since. Shepherds moved into the village never to return to their isolated homes.

Farmers did make money - wool was in demand for uniforms and bulk food for troops (not quality). There was a price however. The rural people worked all day on the land and with the Home Guard or Fire Watching at night. This put great pressure on their health. A friend is sure this is why his Father died early in life. The older men and women did a lot of the work on the farms, the younger ones being in the forces. Boys helped too.

People cycled to work past us daily. We never knew what most of them were doing until years later. We would say, "How do?" and occasionally they would help us pull a sheep out of a ditch. Some worked at the Radar Station and were billeted in Rye. After the war we found evidence of a deception scheme around the Marsh - a dummy airfield, wooden aircraft with lights shining deliberately and so on. Two older men used to cycle out between here and Lydd. There they nailed a few boards and moved things around just to keep the enemy guessing.

There were anti-personnel bombs. As kids at school and at home, we were lectured severely by Police and parents not to touch any unusual objects: to be alert. One thing caused a real alarm. I was walking the dogs by a ditch - near one of the armoured cars and I saw a silver, spherical, smooth and shiny object which bubbled as it bobbed about! Eventually after investigation - it turned out to be a broken Thermos Flask, which had been thrown away by someone working on the other side of the ditch! We used to pick up the shrapnel, used shell cases, bomb splinters etc - it was good fun. The Perspex canopies from crashed aircraft were much in demand and swapped at school. Shrapnel was a nuisance in the fields - as it got into the mowing machines and blunted the knives.

Our sheep were sold in Rye Market to the Ministry of Agriculture. Cattle and sheep were dealt with and many went away by train. There were two Corn Stores, Stonham's at the foot of Mermaid Street and Harry Thorpe on Ferry Road. Ours went to Stonham's. Gaol was the punishment for those selling illegally. I was not involved in decisions about buying and selling, as I was too young. The workmen knew me only as 'the boy'.

There was a Black Market for petrol, petrol coupons, food etc. My Father was horrified when he was offered a tractor. We were desperate for machinery and this one was on rubber tyres, had a self-starter and lights. He suddenly realised it was stolen from an airfield! There were no takers in East Guldeford - we were only too glad not to have been invaded and to have survived alive.

Father did allow a little barter system e.g. rabbits for favours. He had a rapport with the Telephone Exchange. He was on the phone a lot at night - it was the old plug-in type of exchange and he got to know one of the men, as it was always the same one on duty. He said if he liked to come down he would give him a few eggs. There were very few phones - ours was the only one on the East Guldeford corner. If any traffic broke down, they used ours.

There was a terrible shortage of paper, string, and metal; there was no soft loo paper or wrapping paper. Envelopes were always re-used and waste paper was saved. Newspapers were only ever two pages long.

There were poster campaigns, to be careful of "Careless Talk" etc. Parcels from relations in Australia made our Christmas. They always had a fruitcake sent in the tin in which it had been baked, dried fruit that was unheard of in the war, and woollen items.

On V.E.Day evening we cycled in to see the Celebrations. There were a few flags in the High Street but not a soul about, and I was too young to be taken to a pub! The atmosphere was one of great relief - not of celebration that the war was over: things could only get better!

Recollections of Mr. Moppett P.C. of War in Rye

as told to the T.P.C.C.Local History Group in 1989

I came to Rye in July 1939 and, at this time, I lived at Church Square Police Station. I served for 30 years in the Sussex Police, being stationed at Lewes, East Grinstead and Rye, then as the village policeman at Northiam and Pevensey, and I finished my career at Battle as a Sergeant. I have been retired for 23 years. My Father was a London Policeman and I was born there, but my family moved to Mayfield. I wasn't allowed to serve there, as the Police are always against you working where you have relatives - for fear of bias.

Soon after the beginning of the war, I was the only regular Constable in Rye, working with a Sergeant, an Inspector and some Specials - all the other policemen had been called up as war reserves. As Rye was small, the Police and civilians could manage it. I was the last Constable to live at the Old Police Station in Church Square, before it was bombed in August 1940. The police house was a tremendous size and it was cold and draughty. It had three cells at the back, which were separate from it. After bomb damage was repaired, it was converted into offices.

There were three cells in the Ypres Tower, which we could use, and also a Mortuary on the bottom floor of this Tower, where all of the dead bodies - including both German and Allied airmen who had been shot down - were taken. I had to inspect the bodies and tell the Coroner when someone had died. In those days, in a case of sudden death, the Policeman was the Coroner's Officer. The military personnel had their own department for dealing with the bodies, but I had to see that arrangements were made to lay them out, and in the case of Irish Roman Catholics, for embalming before burial. I had to deal with sackfuls of bodies - such as two German sailors who were washed ashore from a submarine, and an Irish soldier, shot through the forehead on his way from Udimore to Rye and a German airman shot down on the Marsh (the crew were injured and taken to Rye Hospital, but the pilot died there). I had to search them for identification - on one was a ticket for a Paris Theatre for that night's performance! On another, from one of our Blenheim's that had been shot down, came a lovely English leather wallet. These had to be returned to the families eventually. On the other hand, I had to go round in Rye and district and tell families when their boys had been killed away from home - this was an awful job.

To return to my story, when war broke out I was on Lewes Railway Station escorting a German woman who had been living in Rye, to Holloway Prison. We Police had an Aliens List of those who were thought to have something in their background, which might be dangerous to our security. As there were no Policewomen in those days, my wife had to accompany me as escort. I got the impression that this German woman was "not innocent" for, as we passed Newhaven, where we could see the British Navy at work - coal boats, six destroyers etc., she was very knowledgeable about them and she seemed very "hard".

My job usually ranged between an eight and twelve hour day with no increase in pay for extra hours. I was told I was expected to work for twenty-five hours a day! I, like Policemen in the villages, had a B.S.A. cycle, the sergeant at Battle had a motor cycle and the Inspector at Rye had his own car, for which he was paid an allowance for official use. In order to communicate with others, for example if there was an accident and we needed an ambulance, we had to look for a telephone wire, follow it to a house and ask to use it, or stop a car and get a message to the Station that way!

On the beat, we used the ordinary G.P.O. telephone box. We had to phone in every half hour. The boxes were outside Horrell's on the High Street, on the Railway Approach, at the Strand, on Cadborough Road, and in Bedford Place.

The first few months of the war were quiet, just a few bombers flying over.

There were certain War Precautions that I was involved in enforcing in Rye. The Police had the power to stop anyone and check their Identity Card at any time. After the fall of France, the situation was bad and the whole South East coast to Bournemouth was a prohibited area for civilians. I had to make flash checks on the Railway station and sometimes I got aggravation. If you did not have your card on you there was trouble - and you had to bring it to the Station within five days even if we knew something about you. About the time of D Day in 1944 things were even more closed here - checks were made more closely. Soldiers were not allowed to have their wives and children in the area because the Regiments were preparing for going abroad and soldiers were not allowed to visit their families. Any wives already here were cleared out. One Captain I remember had his wife at Northiam and he never revealed that she was there. He was found out, was arrested and reduced to the ranks.

During the evacuation time in 1940, when it seemed the Germans might invade, I had the job of going round to all essential personnel to compel them to stay in Rye - even if the Germans had landed - I had to serve a notice on them. They included all the Fire Brigade, the Home Guard and Civil Defence.

Rye was a wonderful place in the war - it was like a land of the "quick and the dead". Many had evacuated and yet there were about 2000 troops living here in the town. The Billeting Officer looked at all the big houses, which were empty, assessed their size in square feet, and then allocated the soldiers to them. The Regimental H.Q. was at Cadborough - I remember rationing was very strict for us civilians but not for the troops - and one night, on patrol up Cadborough about 3 am, I called in on the Canadian troops, to see them opening a huge tin of corned beef - they offered me some. (The aim of rationing was to let us have the minimum amount of food so that if the German troops landed, we couldn't feed them.)

The Food Office was in Ferry Road where ration books, etc. were distributed. We stored spare ones - they were locked in the back of the Police Station.

I dealt with the soldiers when they had committed civil crimes - for example one soldier was fined for a breach of law for carrying a gun when off duty. There were probably 3000 between Rye and Winchelsea - some good, others bad and still others indifferent! Generally there was a good feeling between the soldiers and the townsfolk. There were competitions between them in cricket and football on the Salts. I felt sorry when the Cinema was bombed, (the bomb caused the building to fall inwards into a pile of rubble and it killed the manager), as all had enjoyed visits to it.

Another job I had was to check blackout - there was always somebody showing a light!

After the fall of the Low Countries in 1940, several boats came to Rye from there. One Dutch barge came to Strand Quay with five or six people on it - and a beautiful big dog. This wasn't allowed ashore because of the danger of rabies, but the boat stayed for some time - I had to keep an eye on its quarantine.

Camber was a prohibited area - no one without a pass was allowed. I had a pass. The residents had been allowed varying times to move out - some 24 hours, others 72 hours. The Military took over and it became an encampment and the Military Police were in charge there.

They laid minefields all the way from Camber to Rye. I remember one German fighter (and there were a lot of them), having run out of fuel, sitting in the middle of one of these fields. The pilot had been taken out and was sitting to attention on a chair in a hut. He was shouting "Heil Hitler!" and demanding to speak to the nearest German Officer. He was taken to Prison Camp after interrogation. I had lots of very subdued Germans in the Police Station before they were sent away.

Winchelsea Beach towards Pett was flooded as a last precaution against Jerry. All the marshes had hop poles with wire strung between them. This was to stop planes and paratroopers landing. One plane did come down in a big field about a mile from the coast and the wires cut the pilot's head off.

After Dunkirk, the Army had very little transport and it was thought that Jerry would land here in the southeast, that they would land by parachute and would dive bomb. Many lorries were confiscated and it was decided to have a Cycle Platoon on Romney Marsh and in Rye. All bicycles were to be brought to the Police Station - 120 at once! Where they thought we were going to put them I don't know. The Sergeant said to me "You're off duty for a fortnight. Take this clip board and foolscap paper and go round to every door and list all the cycles in Rye." Most houses in Rye had a father or son away at the front and so had a spare bike in the shed doing nothing. The Government paid for them - whatever the householder asked - £3, £4 or £5 - we never queried the cost. I went to Odell's, the cycle shop on Market Road, and bought up all his stock. Mrs B....... had a B.S.A. Roadster and she hid behind the curtains!

A week later two Army lorries came and loaded up all the bikes, including tradesmen's bikes - these would hold a box of ammunition! This platoon lasted for about four or five weeks and then the invasion scare faded out.

I remember I had to go to see one old lady as she had written to the War Office to say, "Get rid of the guns in the Gun Garden because the Germans will think it is a fortified town!"

Another memory is of an evacuee - I was in Ferry Road and I saw a boy sitting on a wall, which was overhung with an apple tree. He was greedily eating apples. I coughed and said "What are you doing son?" He didn't run but said "Eating apples." He had never seen an apple tree before and thought anyone could have them - it was just a different style of living.

We could actually see the smoke all over the French coast, when the Battle of Dunkirk was raging, from our garden. It lasted a week whilst we were evacuating and burning our equipment. We could see the bombs going over the French coast - we counted 15 from first seeing the plane, to seeing the bombs, until they landed on Boulogne.

Radar was our salvation and I saw our Station [*by the Kent Ditch. Ed.*] dive-bombed. The planes were picked up coming, before they left France and coming over the Channel and gave us a ten-minute warning. They missed - I suppose it was a small target from 10,000 ft.

I believe they did hit one in West Sussex. We never knew how radar worked and there were all sorts of rumours in the winter before the war, when the Station was being built so urgently in the snow. Things were said like, "It's to fire rockets!"

I watched the Battle of Britain dogfights - they were specks in the sky! There would then be a flame and then a parachute. Ten minutes of excitement watching it come down, was followed by me having to go to pick up the remains. On one occasion I found a beautiful German Spandau machine gun, which had been shot off a plane.

Cannon shells were strewn about - they were half an inch long of thick plate steel. I went round putting them into my gas mask case, which was lined with cotton wool. On one occasion two banged together and blew a hole in it!

The first German bomb fell bang in the centre of the town in June 1940 and there were several later on. I went to help after bombs had fallen - I often saw then from my garden. I recall when big Jerry bombs fell on a row of council houses; there was just dust and rubble everywhere and much damage had been done by stones coming down. One woman was killed in this way.

In the raid, which damaged the Pipemaker's Arms, six cottages were knocked down and three people were killed and three were injured. It is surprising however, that so few were killed in Rye.

Another fell on the Ypres Tower. I had been on night duty and had finished at 6 am. I was due on again at 2 pm and so got up at 12.30 pm. At 12.40 pm the bomb fell - and my bed was full of arrows of glass - I would have been cut badly if I had still been in it. My six-month-old daughter was normally in her pram in the back yard and this was six inches deep in rubble when it was brought in! She was unhurt.

Other scenes I attended were when oil bombs fell on Rye Harbour one night, and when incendiary bombs were dropped. There were about 100 of these incendiary bombs in a canister like a dustbin. This would open on contact with the ground and the bombs run out. These bombs would set anything alight! The ARP had just a stirrup pump to cope with them. Later in the war, one in ten would contain an explosive shell. We would have to stand back for ten minutes after the fire was burning to see if it would explode.

I was in Northiam when the Flying Bomb/Doodlebugs came over - they got more and more daily - up to 100 a day. Twelve actually fell in Northiam. The first night they went over we didn't know what they were like - in fact they were jet propelled, like a small aeroplane, and contained 1000lbs of explosive. We had no warning, as these V 1's went faster than sound. We could actually see them go up from the French coast, but then lost sight of them. Our guns couldn't touch them as they were too fast, flew too low and were too heavily protected. The Ack Ack guns were brought from London to put along the coast from Camber to Kent, backed up with fighter planes over the Channel. We in Northiam were behind these lines defended by the fighter planes and we had some barrage balloons - the aim was not to let them get to London. A higher-powered Mosquito fighter was introduced after six - ten weeks and the attacks tapered off.

I recall that Major Hacking in the Home Guard in Rye was later killed with a bomb. In Northiam Captain Cyster was in charge.
I heard that the war had ended on the radio at 9 am - it said that the war would finish at 11/12 o'clock that morning. I remember noticing that the following Sunday all the lights were on in the church!

In this Police area there were over 400 medals for gallantry presented - including three Kings' Police Medals. These last were to men in East London, Ashford and Superintendent, later Inspector, Wickens in Rye.

Civilian Gas Mask cases.

FRANK PALMER JR

Whilst staying with my grandfather during the school holidays, I witnessed many 'Doodlebugs' passing over or near Rye. The gunfire was deafening with many hundreds of shells being fired in an attempt to destroy those flying bombs. Many were successful, as were some fighter aircraft with the same mission, but some still got through these outer defences.

On Tuesday 29th August 1944 I visited Rock Channel Shipyard with my father. We were being taken over a Motor Fishing Vessel (a wooden mine sweeper built tot look like a fishing boat), being built for the Royal Navy.

Whilst on the deck of this M.F.V., a 'Doodlebug' appeared; the guns opened up and it was knocked off course by this gunfire. It went into a vertical climb until out of sight, and then it turned and came down in a steep dive and it appeared to me, straight towards the shipyard. The men working on the boat all dived for cover. My father and I joined them crouching low on the deck. I remember thinking I could almost touch it! Then it did a little loop, turned back towards the sea, and crashed on the beach with a loud explosion.

That day I saw 23 'Doodlebugs' (18 during the day and 5 at night). Of these, guns exploded 6 and a further 6 were brought down either by guns or fighters, but 11 got through these outer defences.
This was almost the last of the 'Doodlebugs' in the S.E. I saw one brought down by guns during darkness the following day. On the last day of August and the 1st of September there were no sightings.

FRANK PALMER SR.

In June 1944, the first 'Doodlebug' was spotted and hundreds of guns were brought south, in fact it was the biggest concentration of artillery in the country and the cannonade was terrific. I was thistle-spudding with my father-in-law at Leasam, when, hearing the sirens go off, we both jumped down in the ditch as two 'Doodles' went over. [*From R.M.'When I was Young'*]

BOROUGH OF RYE
Summary of Enemy Action

Within the boundaries of the above district the following enemy action has been experienced up to the 30th November 1944

Alerts	1472 (15 of these were 'local')
Incidents	38
High explosive bombs	88
Oil bombs	I
Incendiary bombs (approx.No.)	200
Flying bombs	7
Crashed enemy aircraft	-
Machine gun and cannon fire incidents	17
Mines	I
(outside Borough but caused damage inside)	
Other missiles	I

CASUALTIES

Killed	12
Died in hospital	3
severely injured	26
Slightly injured	54

DAMAGE TO PROPERTY.

	Dwelling Houses	Other Premises	Total
(I) Totally destroyed	55	9	64
(2) Severely damaged but capable of repair	282	53	335
(3) Slightly damaged	924	133	1057
Many premises under (2) and (3) damaged several times giving total incidents of damage	2536	324	2860

In addition to the above inside the Borough of Rye, the C.D. General Services of the Borough of Rye attended numerous incidents for the Battle R.D.C. in Playden, Iden, Peasmarsh, Camber, Rye Harbour, Icklesham, Winchelsea and Udimore on approximately 30 incidents and in addition attended in those areas some 9 crashed British Aircraft, and 2 enemy. Services involved were Wardens, Rescue, Ambulance and First Aid Post. Casualties were brought to Rye First Aid Post in many instances and the dead to the Rye Mortuary.
Numerous gun and searchlight sites for the Army were covered in the area in and around Rye and casualties dealt with on various occasions.

ARTHUR G.J.CORNNER. 10, High Street, Rye
Sub-Controller. 14th December,
1944

Home Guard marching through Rye

BIBLIOGRAPHY AND FOR MORE INFORMATION

Angell, Stewart The Secret Sussex Resistance Middleton Press 1996
Kirkham, Josephine Ed. Rye Memories 25 Volumes Thomas Peacocke Community College 1985 - 1996

INDEX